CHILDREN'S
ENCYCLOPEDIA
OF ANIMALS

Michael Leach and Meriel Lland

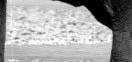

ARCTURUS

ARCTURUS

This edition published in 2021 by Arcturus Publishing Limited
26/27 Bickels Yard, 151–153 Bermondsey Street,
London SE1 3HA

Copyright © Arcturus Holdings Limited

Authors: Michael Leach and Meriel Lland
Editor: Clare Hibbert @ Hollow Pond
Designer: Amy McSimpson @ Hollow Pond

ISBN: 978-1-78828-506-3
CH005810NT
Supplier 29, Date 0121, Print run 11116

Printed in China

CHILDREN'S ENCYCLOPEDIA OF ANIMALS

CONTENTS

INTRODUCTION 4

CHAPTER ONE
Mammals: Carnivores 6
CATS 8
WOLVES 10
FOXES 12
BEARS 14
THE SEAL FAMILY 16
WHALES AND DOLPHINS 18
BATS 20
OTTERS 22
MONGOOSES 24

CHAPTER TWO
Mammals: Omnivores
and Herbivores 26
ELEPHANTS 28
RHINOS 30
GIRAFFES 32
CAMELS 34
APES 36
MONKEYS AND LEMURS 38
MARSUPIALS 40
RODENTS 42
WILD PIGS 44

CHAPTER THREE
Birds 46
OWLS 48
VULTURES 50
EAGLES 52
SHOWING OFF 54
PARROTS 56
HUMMINGBIRDS 58
PENGUINS 60
WATER BIRDS 62
FLIGHTLESS GIANTS 64

CHAPTER FOUR
Reptiles and Amphibians 66
VENOMOUS SNAKES 68
CONSTRICTORS 70
FROGS 72
TOADS 74
SALAMANDERS 76
TURTLES 78
CHAMELEONS 80
LIZARDS 82
CROCODILES 84

CHAPTER FIVE
Sea Creatures 86
FISH 88
SHARKS 90
CEPHALOPODS 92
SEAHORSES 94
CRABS AND LOBSTERS 96
CORAL REEFS 98
THE DEEP 100
JELLYFISH 102
SEA STARS 104

CHAPTER SIX: Minibeasts 106
SPIDERS AND SCORPIONS 108
BEETLES 110
SLUGS AND SNAILS 112
BUTTERFLIES 114
BEES 116
THE GRASSHOPPER FAMILY 118
WORMS AND LEECHES 120
ANTS 122
PARASITES 124

GLOSSARY 126
INDEX 128

Introduction

An animal is a living organism made up of cells. It feeds, senses and responds to its surroundings, moves, and reproduces. Scientists have identified nearly nine million species of living animals, but there are many more to be found.

Life Appears

Single-celled life forms appeared around four billion years ago. Sponges—the first animals—appeared a billion years ago. Over time, more complicated animals evolved and some also became extinct. Dinosaurs were the dominant land animals for 165 million years before they died out 65 million years ago.

Fossilized skull of the dinosaur, *Tyrannosaurus rex*

Rhinoceros hornbills are birds that live in Southeast Asian rain forests. Birds are warm-blooded animals with backbones. They have wings and most can fly.

Leaf beetle, an insect

Classifying Life

Scientists organize living things into groups with shared characteristics. The two main kinds of animal are ones with backbones (vertebrates) and ones without (invertebrates). Arthropods make up the biggest invertebrate group. They have segmented bodies and jointed limbs. Insects, spiders, and crabs are all arthropods.

Warm- and Cold-Blooded

Most animals are ectothermic, or "cold-blooded." Their body temperature is controlled by their environment. Mammals and birds are endothermic, or "warm-blooded." Their bodies can generate their own heat, so they can survive in much colder habitats.

Musk ox, a mammal

Langurs in a city

Fragile Earth

We are lucky to share our world with an extraordinary richness of animals. It is important to protect our wildlife. When humans pollute or damage the environment, we harm both animals and people. The future is in our hands.

Animal Habitats

The place where an animal lives is called its habitat. Animals have evolved to inhabit just about every environment on Earth, from tropical rain forests and coral reefs to deserts, mountain tops, and ice floes. They even survive in cities.

Giant leaf–tailed gecko, vulnerable because of habitat loss

Chapter One

Mammals: Carnivores

Mammals are warm-blooded, breathe air, and have a backbone. They give birth to live young, which they feed with mother's milk. Carnivores are mammals that eat meat. Nearly 300 mammal species are true carnivores. They live all over the globe and in all habitats.

Carnivore Features

Carnivorous mammals are built to spot, chase, and kill prey. They have forward-facing eyes that judge distance and long legs for speed. Their large brains help them to hunt strategically. Some carnivores live solitary lives, but others live in packs or groups and hunt as a team.

Carnivores have specialized teeth: long, pointed canines at the front of the mouth for killing and sharp-edged carnassials at the back for slicing through meat.

DID YOU KNOW? Spotted hyenas live in enormous clans of up to 80 animals. They are sometimes called "laughing hyenas" because of their whooping call.

Living Fast

Meat is rich in energy, so carnivores don't need to feed often. When they do hunt, it helps to be in peak condition. Any illness or slight injury slows them. Predators' lives are dangerous and can be short. More predators die of starvation than old age.

A leopard can eat 4 kg (9 lb) of meat at a time. It only needs to hunt twice a week, and can spend the rest of the time resting.

The hyena's crushing bite lets it reach the rich marrow inside bones. Around half of its diet is carrion.

SPOTTED HYENA

CROCUTA CROCUTA

Habitat: Woodlands, grasslands, scrub; sub–Saharan Africa
Length: Male 1.3 m (4.3 ft); female 1.4 m (4.6 ft)
Weight: Male 55 kg (121 lb); female 60 kg (132 lb)
Diet: Mammals
Lifespan: Up to 20 years
Wild population: 40,000; Least Concern

Cats

Cats are carnivores with soft fur, a short snout, and sharp claws. The first cats appeared around 30 million years ago. Today wild cats live everywhere except Australia and the Antarctic. There are 41 wild cat species. Four—the lion, tiger, jaguar, and leopard—are in their own family: the big cats.

Forward–facing eyes let this Bengal tiger judge distance accurately. Most cats are nocturnal hunters and see well in the dark.

Getting a Grip

Cats use their sharp claws to grab prey. In most species the claws retract into the paw when they are not being used. However, the cheetah's claws are always out. They grip the ground and stop the cat slipping when it runs.

The cheetah is the world's fastest mammal. In short bursts it can sprint at 105 km/h (65 mph).

Hearing is a tiger's most important sense. The cat can swivel each ear independently to pick up faraway sounds from all directions.

Long, sensitive whiskers can detect small air movements. This is useful for finding prey at night.

Stripes camouflage tigers in forests and grasslands. Tigers spend an hour every day licking their fur. This removes loose hairs and keeps the coat clean and warm.

The large, sharp canine teeth kill prey. Behind these, the carnassial teeth are used for cutting through flesh.

Family Life

Lions are the only cats that hunt and live in groups. All other species are loners that come together only to breed. Most cats live in forests or grasslands, but some have adapted to other environments. Sand cats live in deserts, hunting birds and lizards and surviving on very little water.

Lions live in family groups called prides. A typical pride includes related lionesses, their cubs, and a couple of adult males.

BENGAL TIGER

PANTHERA TIGRIS "CAT TIGER"

Habitat: Forests, swamps, grasslands; S Asia
Length: Male 3 m (9.8 ft); female 2.6 m (8.5 ft)
Weight: Male 250 kg (551 lb); female 160 kg (353 lb)
Diet: Mammals—e.g. deer, wild pigs
Lifespan: Up to 18 years
Wild population: 2,000–2,500; Endangered

DID YOU KNOW? The largest cat on record was a Siberian tiger that weighed 384 kg (845 lb)—about the same as 90 pet cats!

Wolves

The largest members of the dog family, timber wolves were once the most widely distributed predator on Earth. Today they live only in remote areas of North America and Eurasia, far from humans, but their population is stable. However, the red wolf from the eastern United States and the Ethiopian wolf are both endangered.

Falling Numbers

For centuries, humans hunted wolves because they feared attacks on themselves and their livestock. They also cleared wolves' forest habitats for farmland. Today the timber wolf is extinct in much of Western Europe, Mexico, and the United States.

A timber wolf's coat can be black, white, ash, cream, or brown.

Wolves can smell prey up to 1.6 km (1 mile) away. The nose also tells them whether another wolf is a friend or rival, and whether it has just eaten.

The thick coat is waterproof and warm, thanks to a dense undercoat. Wolves survive at temperatures down to −40°C (−40°F).

DID YOU KNOW? The maned wolf of South America is a member of the dog family, but it is not a true wolf. Most of its diet is made up of fruit and vegetation.

Tails are used for balance and communication. Dominant wolves hold their tail high. Low-ranking animals curl their tail between their legs.

Long legs and stamina mean a wolf can cover 96 km (60 miles) in just six hours. During a chase it can reach 56 km/h (35 mph).

Wolves mark territory by howling and leaving strong-smelling droppings.

Family Affair

A pack's territory can range from just 30 sq km (11.6 sq miles) to as much as 2,000 sq km (770 sq miles). A typical pack contains about a dozen animals. Only the dominant male and female breed. The other pack members work together to protect the cubs.

TIMBER WOLF

CANIS LUPUS
"WOLF DOG"

Habitat: Forests, tundra, mountains, grasslands; N America, Asia, Europe
Length: 3 m (9.8 ft)
Weight: Male 45 kg (99 lb); female 38.5 kg (85 lb)
Diet: Mammals—e.g. deer, buffalo
Lifespan: Up to 12 years
Wild population: Unknown; Least Concern

Foxes

Foxes are the smallest members of the dog family. They have triangular faces, pointed ears, and bushy tails. Intelligent and adaptable, foxes live everywhere except the Antarctic. They have a range of calls, barks, and yelps to communicate fear, warnings, threats, and playfulness.

The highly adaptable red fox lives in cities, woods, mountains, and deserts. It is a hunter and a scavenger.

In cold weather, a red fox covers its body with its long, bushy tail for extra warmth.

Compared to other dogs, foxes are short and stocky. A red fox can jump as far as 2 m (6.5 ft). It is a strong swimmer, too.

RED FOX

VULPES VULPES
"FOX FOX"

Habitat: Forests, farmland, cities, grasslands; Almost worldwide
Length: Male 1.5 m (4.7 ft); female 1.2 m (4 ft)
Weight: Male 12 kg (26.5 lb); female 9.5 kg (21 lb)
Diet: Mammals, birds, insects, reptiles, fruit, garbage
Wild population: Unknown; Least Concern

DID YOU KNOW? Most foxes have 42 teeth, but the bat-eared fox has 48. Its teeth are extremely pointy and help it crunch up termites and other minibeasts.

The red fox uses its senses of hearing and smell to pinpoint the position of prey animals.

Unlike most dogs, a fox cannot bare its teeth.

Skilled Survivor

The 12 "true foxes" include red foxes, Arctic foxes, and kit foxes. The red fox is the most widespread carnivore. It eats anything, from invertebrates and small mammals to grasses and kitchen waste. Foxes bury stashes of food in times of plenty and then return to them when they are hungry.

The Arctic fox has adapted to live in the cold north. Its winter coat is white to blend in with the snow.

Desert Dweller

The smallest wild dog is the fennec fox, which lives in the driest parts of North Africa. It stays cool by losing excess body heat through its huge ears. The ears also funnel sounds so that the fox can locate prey at night and underground. Prey provides most of the fox's moisture.

The fennec fox is the smallest wild dog. Standing only 20 cm (8 in) tall, it is about the same size as a pet kitten.

Bears

There are eight species of bear. They live in Asia, Europe, and the Americas. Most are omnivores that feed on plants and insects and live in forest habitats. They only eat meat if they find carrion or a slow-moving, weak animal. Polar bears are the exception. These speedy hunters are carnivores.

The Bear's Year

Polar bears are active all year round, but other bears in the far north—grizzlies and black bears—hibernate in winter. In warmer places, there is plenty of food all year. Species such as Indian sloth bears don't need a winter sleep.

Underneath the dense, waterproof fur is a thick layer of fatty blubber to protect the polar bear from the cold.

When salmon swim upriver to breed in late summer, grizzlies have a fishy feast! It helps them put on weight ready for hibernation.

Bears are usually loners, but mothers look after their cubs for two years or more. The cubs grow quickly because their mother's milk is about one-third fat.

POLAR BEAR

URSUS MARITIMUS
"SEA BEAR"

Habitat: Tundra, ice floes, oceans; Arctic
Length: Male 2.8 m (9.2 ft);
 female 2.4 m (7.2 ft)
Weight: Male 600 kg (1,323 lb);
 female 260 kg (573 lb)
Diet: Seals, carrion, fish
Lifespan: Up to 25 years
Wild population: 30,000; Vulnerable

All bears have amazingly sensitive noses. They can smell food up to 50 km (30 miles) away.

Picky Pandas

Most bears eat many kinds of food, but pandas are choosy. Ninety-nine percent of their diet is bamboo. Pandas live in the mountains of China. They are threatened by habitat loss and only around 1,500 are left in the wild.

The bear's pale, creamy coat helps to camouflage it against the snow.

Most mammals are digitigrade—they walk on their toes. Bears (and humans) are plantigrade—they stand on the soles of their feet.

Pandas spend most of their waking hours eating. They eat about 600 bamboo stems a day.

DID YOU KNOW? The smallest bear is the sun bear. It grows no bigger than a ten-year-old child, but its tongue is an amazing 25 cm (10 in) long!

15

The Seal Family

The zoological name for seals and their relatives is pinnipeds, which means "fin-foot." Their webbed back feet provide the power for swimming, while the front legs are used for walking—clumsily!—on land. Seals, sea lions, and walruses all live in cool water and avoid tropical seas.

In their Element

Underwater, seals pursue prey at speeds up to 27 km/h (17 mph), thanks to their streamlined bodies. However, like all marine mammals, they must surface to breathe. Elephant seals hold their breath longest— their dives last 100 minutes or more.

The common seal is a true or earless seal. It does not have external ear flaps.

Large eyes can see well in the low light levels underwater.

The Weddell seal lives in Antarctic waters. It can dive as deep as 600 m (2,000 ft).

The nostrils completely close when the seal is diving. The animal has a good sense of smell on land.

Whiskers sense tiny movements in the water, helping the seal locate prey when it is too dark to see.

DID YOU KNOW? The Saimaa ringed seal is the rarest pinniped. It is found in only one lake in Finland, and the total population is just 320.

A thick layer of blubber beneath the skin insulates the seal (keeps it warm) and aids buoyancy.

Pinnipeds in Danger

The pinnipeds are made up of three families: true or earless seals, eared seals (sea lions and fur seals), and walruses. Almost a third are at risk, threatened mainly by climate change and pollution. In the past, many fur seals were hunted close to extinction for their fur.

In the past, walruses have been hunted for their ivory tusks. Today, the trade in ivory is illegal.

COMMON SEAL

PHOCA VITULINA
"CALF–LIKE SEAL"

Habitat: North Sea, Baltic, N Atlantic, N Pacific
Length: Male 1.8 m (5.9 ft);
 female 1.6 m (5.2 ft)
Weight: Male 120 kg (265 lb);
 female 90 kg (198 lb)
Diet: Seals, carrion, fish
Lifespan: Up to 20 years
Wild population: 350,000; Least Concern

Whales and Dolphins

Dolphins and whales are cetaceans—highly intelligent mammals that mate, feed, and give birth in all the world's oceans. Cetaceans are split into two groups: baleen whales, which eat invertebrates, and toothed whales, such as dolphins, which take much bigger prey.

Filter-Feeders

Blue whales, humpbacks, and other baleen whales are filter-feeders. These huge animals have sieve-like plates inside their mouths to filter plankton, krill, or other foods from the water.

This is a baby humpback whale. Baby whales drink the equivalent of one-and-a-third bathtubfuls of mother's milk a day!

COMMON DOLPHIN

DELPHINUS DELPHIS
"DOLPHIN DOLPHIN"

Habitat: Atlantic, Pacific, Indian Ocean, Mediterranean Sea
Length: Male 2.2 m (7.2 ft); female 2.1 m (6.9 ft)
Weight: Male 120 kg (265 lb); female 105 kg (231 lb)
Diet: Fish, squid, octopus
Lifespan: Around 20 years
Wild population: Unknown: Least Concern

DID YOU KNOW? Blue whales are the largest animals that have ever lived on Earth. Adults can be 27 m (89 ft) long and weigh more than 145 tonnes (160 tons).

Dolphins travel in pods of up to 1,000. They live mainly in warm waters, hunting fish and squid.

The dolphins herded the fish into a ball shape. It is easy to pick off individuals from the edge of the ball.

Finding Food

Dolphins and other toothed whales use echolocation to navigate and find prey. They produce clicks that travel through the water and then bounce back to them off objects. Cetaceans also use noises to communicate with each other. Humpbacks are known for their long, complex songs.

The orca is the largest species of dolphin. It mostly hunts seals, but also eats squid, sea birds, fish, and even turtles.

Bats

There are around 1,100 living species of bats, making up about one-fifth of all mammal species. They live worldwide apart from in the frozen Arctic and Antarctic. Bats are the only mammals that have evolved true powered flight. Other "flying" mammals, such as the flying squirrel, can only glide.

Batty Diets

Seventy percent of bats feed on insects. One brown bat ate 1,000 mosquitoes in an hour! Bats have adapted to hunt other sources of meat, such as birds, frogs, lizards, fish, or other bats. Vampire bats are famous for drinking blood from cows, horses, or sheep. The largest bats, called megabats or flying foxes, feed on fruit.

The spectral vampire bat is the world's largest carnivorous bat. It feeds on small birds and reptiles.

The greater bulldog bat is a fishing bat. It uses its feet to snatch fish or insects from lakes or rivers.

Bat Senses

Bats have keen eyesight and a good sense of smell. However, most bats find food using echolocation. They send out high-frequency sound waves, then listen to how the waves bounce back off objects. From this, the bats can work out an object's exact position, size, and shape.

By hanging upside-down, bats can drop into the air and then fly. It takes less energy than taking off upward like a bird.

DID YOU KNOW? The world's biggest bat is the giant golden-crowned flying fox from the Philippines. It weighs 1.2 kg (2.6 lb) and has a 1.7-m (5.6-ft) wingspan.

The wings are thin skin stretched over thin bones. Sleeping bats wrap their wings around themselves for warmth.

Flying foxes live in tropical forests. They do not have echolocation. They use eyesight and smell to find flowers and fruit to eat.

LYLE'S FLYING FOX

PTEROPUS LYLEI

Habitat: Forests, farmland, cities; SE Asia
Length: 22 cm (8.7 in)
Wingspan: 90 cm (35.4 in)
Weight: 390 g (0.9 lb)
Diet: Ripe fruit, nectar
Lifespan: Up to 20 years
Wild population: Unknown; Decreasing

DID YOU KNOW? Sea otters sleep in groups, called rafts, of up to 100 animals. They hold paws and wrap strands of seaweed around their bodies so they don't drift away.

22

Otters

The 13 otter species are members of the mustelid family, along with badgers, wolverines, and weasels. These predators are found everywhere except Australia and the Antarctic. Otters have slim, streamlined bodies, short legs, webbed feet, and a strong tail.

Clever with Clams

Sea otters are one of the few mammals that use tools. When feeding on shellfish, a sea otter swims on its back and balances a flat stone on its chest. Grasping the prey in its front paws, it smashes open the shell on the rock.

Sea otters can weigh up to 45 kg (99 lb). A very thick coat of fur keeps them warm in their ocean home.

The otter makes many different calls and whistles to communicate.

The Eurasian otter lives in fresh water and along coasts.

The longest mustelid is the endangered giant otter, which lives in South America. It can be up to 1.7 m (5.6 ft) long.

Long, sensitive whiskers can find food by touch.

Otter Basics

For otters, the main diet is fish, but they will eat almost any small animal. Apart from the sea otters, all species hunt both in water and on land, in daylight or darkness. Most are very territorial and mark their home range with piles of smelly droppings called spraint.

The otter's head is flat, with the nose and eyes high on the skull. When it swims, only the very top of the head is visible.

EURASIAN OTTER

LUTRA LUTRA
"OTTER OTTER"

Habitat: Lakes, rivers, coasts; Europe, Asia
Length: Male 1.3 m (4.3 ft); female 1.1 m (3.6 ft)
Weight: Male 10 kg (22 lb); female 7 kg (15.4 lb)
Diet: Fish, amphibians, crustaceans
Lifespan: Up to 10 years
Wild population: Unknown; Near Threatened

DID YOU KNOW? Snake venom does not affect mongooses. A 5-kg (11-lb) mongoose would not even notice a cobra bite that would kill a human!

24

Mongooses

Mongooses are native to Africa and India. Although they look like weasels, mongooses are more closely related to cats. Most mongooses are omnivores—their main food is meat, but they also take plants, insects, and eggs.

Social or Solitary?

Most mongoose species are solitary animals. Others, including meerkats, yellow mongooses, and banded mongooses, live in social groups called colonies. Living together lets them share different jobs, such as building burrows, hunting for food, bringing up kits, and keeping a look out for predators.

This banded mongoose is acting as sentinel. If it spots an eagle, jackal, or other predator, it will warn the rest of the colony.

Meerkats are mongooses adapted to survive in the dry habitats of southern Africa. They live in family groups of up to 30 animals.

Meerkats mostly eat insects, but they also hunt scorpions, lizards, snakes, and small birds.

Excellent senses and fast reflexes make meerkats very successful hunters.

The legs are short enough to move in underground burrows, but fast enough to run at a top speed of 48 km/h (30 mph).

This yellow mongoose has been fortunate enough to kill a small bird. Its usual diet is insects, spiders, and scorpions.

Natural Born Killers

Mongooses have been introduced to islands around the world to control overpopulations of rats and mice. However, mongooses are such good hunters that they have killed local wildlife as well as the pests. It is now illegal to introduce them into new countries.

Meerkats and other mongooses have long, sharp claws for digging. They build underground burrows where they sleep and give birth.

MEERKAT
SURICATA SURICATTA

Habitat: Deserts: S Africa
Length: Male 50 cm (20 in); female 45 cm (17.7 in)
Weight: Male 750 g (26.5 oz); female 720 g (25.4 oz)
Diet: Insects, arachnids, reptiles, small birds
Lifespan: Up to 12 years
Wild population: Unknown; Least Concern

Chapter Two

Mammals: Omnivores and Herbivores

Some mammals eat both meat and plants. These are the omnivores, adaptable species that survive on a wide variety of food. Herbivores are specialists that eat only vegetation—leaves, grass, flowers, bark, and other plant parts.

PLAINS ZEBRA

EQUUS QUAGGA

Habitat: Forests, grasslands, scrub; E & S Africa
Length: Male 2.3 m (7.5 ft); female 2 m (6.6 ft)
Weight: Male 300 kg (661 lb); female 250 kg (551 lb)
Diet: Grass, low-growing plants
Lifespan: Up to 25 years
Wild population: 750,000; Near Threatened

DID YOU KNOW? Hippos eat up to 35 kg (77 lb) of grass a day—but these "herbivores" will also kill and eat impalas (antelopes).

Varied Diet

Omnivores have more choice than specialists. They can eat foods that are in season and change their diet if a particular food source dries up.

A badger feasts on fruit when it is in season, eats worms when it's raining, and catches small mammals when it can.

Zebra and wildebeest are herbivores. Grazers have sharp front teeth called incisors to snip off plants, and big, flat back teeth called molars for chewing.

Digestive Challenges

Plants are hard to digest. Some animals, such as rabbits, get around this by eating their droppings. As the food passes through the body a second time, they absorb any remaining goodness. Other animals simply take a long time to process their food.

Food passes through the human body in about 30 hours, but in a sloth this can take up to three weeks!

27

Elephants

Elephants evolved 50 million years ago. The two kinds alive today are African and Asian elephants. They live in family groups of up to 12 females and their calves, led by an older female called the matriarch. Adult male elephants live alone or in male-only herds.

African or Asian?

The African elephant is the world's largest land animal. One male weighed 11,000 kg (24,000 lb). Asian elephants are smaller and have smaller ears. Their backs are flat or humped; the African elephant's back has a dip in the middle.

Elephant babies take longer to develop inside their mother than any other land mammal. The mother elephant is pregnant for 22 months.

The front teeth, or tusks, dig up roots and strip bark from trees. Inside the mouth, four huge molars grind up plant food.

The ears are used as fans to cool the elephant on hot days. Each elephant can be identified by the shape and size of its ears.

ASIAN ELEPHANT

ELEPHAS MAXIMUS
"LARGEST OX"

Habitat: Forests, scrub; S Asia
Length: Male 3 m (9.8 ft);
  female 2.7 m (8.9 ft)
Weight: Male 4,500 kg (9,921 lb);
  female 2,750 kg (6,063 lb)
Diet: Leaves, twigs, bark
Lifespan: Up to 60 years
Wild population: 40,000; Endangered

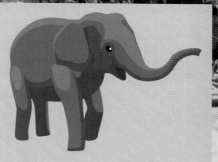

Trunk Talk

The elephant's trunk is an extension of its nose and top lip. It is incredibly sensitive and versatile. It can carry food and water into the mouth, squirt water, or spray dust. It is also used to touch and stroke.

Elephants suck up dust and then blow it over their back and shoulders. It acts as a sunscreen and keeps away insects.

The tail is 1.3 m (4 ft) long and tipped with long, thick hair. It can be flicked like a fly swat to drive away insects.

The trunk is so complicated that it takes a calf a year to master using it! It can grasp, suck, touch, and smell.

DID YOU KNOW? An elephant's trunk has more than 40,000 muscles. The whole human body contains fewer than 1,000 muscles!

29

Rhinos

The rhinoceros is the second-largest land animal after the elephant. It has a sturdy body, tough skin, and one or two defensive horns. There are five species. The white rhino and black rhino both live in Africa. The Indian, Javan, and Sumatran rhinos live in Asia.

Rhino Communications

Scent is very important for rhinos. The largest part of their brain is devoted to processing it, and they mark their territory with dung and urine. Rhinos also use sound to communicate. They make an assortment of noises including squeals, snorts, growls, and moos.

The black rhino lives in dry grasslands in eastern Africa. It feeds on twigs, shoots, and leaves.

Its extremely thick, hairless skin means the rhino overheats easily. Wallowing in mud is a good way to cool down, and the dried mud helps to stop sunburn.

WHITE RHINOCEROS

CERATOTHERIUM SIMUM

"HORNED BEAST WITH A FLAT NOSE"

Habitat: Grasslands; E & S Africa
Length: Male 4 m (13 ft); female 3.6 m (11.8 ft)
Weight: Male 2,500 kg (5512 lb); female 2,000 kg (4,409 lb)
Diet: Grass, low–growing plants
Lifespan: Up to 50 years
Wild population: 20,000; Vulnerable

DID YOU KNOW? Rhinos move fast in spite of their bulk. Black and Indian rhinos are the speediest—they can charge at 55 km/h (34 mph).

Rhinos in Danger

All five rhino species are under threat. Some people believe that powdered rhinoceros horn cures diseases. This isn't true, but the belief fuels an illegal trade in rhino horn and causes the slaughter of many animals.

Large, cup-shaped ears can swivel to pick up sounds from all around. Rhinos can even detect sounds when they are asleep.

Conservationists deliberately removed this Indian bull rhino's horn. They hope this will stop him being targeted by poachers.

Rhinoceros means "nose horn." The horn is made of keratin, the same substance that makes our hair and nails.

Rhinos have small eyes and poor eyesight. They only see well at close range. Anything more than 10 m (33 ft) away is out of focus.

Giraffes

The giraffe is the world's tallest animal, standing up to 5.7 m (18.7 ft) high. This hoofed mammal lives in female family groups on the African savannah, feeding on twigs and leaves from the treetops. There are nine subspecies, which are distinguished by the patterns of their coats.

Large eyes and great height give the giraffe excellent vision.

Both male and female giraffes have short horns covered in bristly hairs. The males butt these when they spar for dominance.

Like our fingerprints, no two giraffes have exactly the same markings.

Standing Tall

Giraffe calves can stand and walk within an hour of being born. They spend their lives standing up, and even sleep on their feet. Giraffes gallop at up to 48 km/h (30 mph) and look graceful—unless they are drinking. Their legs are shorter than their neck, so they bend down very awkwardly!

A drinking giraffe is very vulnerable. It takes a while to stand back up straight again.

The giraffe can use its 46 cm/18 in-long tongue to grip a plant while its teeth strip off the leaves.

Zebra or Giraffe?

The okapi is a close cousin of the giraffe but it lacks the long neck and has a zebra's stripes. Hunted for its unusual and beautiful skin, as well as for meat, the okapi is endangered today. Its forest home is also threatened by illegal mining and logging.

Zebra-like stripes on the okapi's rear and legs provide camouflage in its rain forest habitat.

GIRAFFE

GIRAFFA CAMELOPARDALIS
"FAST-WALKING CAMEL LEOPARD"

Habitat: Savannah, forests; E & S Africa
Length: Male 5.5 m (18 ft); female 4.8 m (15.7 ft)
Weight: Male 1,200 kg (2,646 lb); female 830 kg (1,830 lb)
Diet: Leaves, twigs, bark
Lifespan: Up to 25 years
Wild population: Unknown; Vulnerable

DID YOU KNOW? Giraffes and humans have the same number of bones in their neck—seven. Each giraffe vertebra can be 25 cm (10 in) long.

Camels

There are two camel species: the one-humped dromedary and the two-humped Bactrian. Both types have been domesticated—used by humans for transportation, and as a source of milk, meat, wool, and leather. There are no wild dromedaries today, but the remaining wild Bactrians live in Central Asia.

Ships of the Desert

Camels are suited to hot, dry environments. They can survive without water for months. They do not overheat, and are able to walk as far as 30 km (19 miles) in a day. At night, when the temperature in the desert drops, their shaggy hair keeps them warm.

Also known as the Arabian camel, the dromedary lives across the Middle East and North Africa.

WILD BACTRIAN CAMEL

CAMELUS FERUS

Habitat: Deserts, dry plains; Mongolia, China
Length: Male 3 m (9.8 ft);
  female 2.6 m (8.5 ft)
Weight: Male 750 kg (1,653 lb);
  female 625 kg (1,378 lb)
Diet: Plants
Lifespan: Up to 40 years
Wild population: 1,000; Critically Endangered

DID YOU KNOW? An angry or fearful camel can bring up its stomach contents to spit at its enemy. The partly digested food has a terrible smell.

Camels' Cousins

Four members of the camel family live in South America. They are sure-footed but do not have humps. Guanacos and vicunas live wild in deserts and highlands. Llamas and alpacas have been domesticated as pack animals and to provide milk, meat, and soft, fleecy wool.

The guanaco is a survivor. Its body can cope in the dry Atacama Desert and at altitudes higher than 4,000 m (13,125 ft).

Long hairs inside the ears keep out sand but still let the camel hear.

Nostrils can close in dust storms. The camel can open them to breathe.

The camel's hump stores fat, not water. This fat can be broken down to provide energy when needed.

Each foot has two hooved toes that spread the weight and stop the camel sinking into the sand.

Apes

The orangutan is the only ape that lives alone instead of in groups. However, a young orangutan stays with its mother for the first eight years of life.

Apes are primates that do not have tails. There are two groups. The great apes are humans, Central Africa's chimpanzees and gorillas, and the orangutan of Borneo and Sumatra. The lesser apes are the 18 gibbon species, which are smaller than their great ape cousins.

Intelligent Beasts

The great apes are large, intelligent animals. They have very advanced brains, great memories, and are good at solving problems. Chimpanzees are the most frequent tool users. They use sticks as "fishing rods" to collect termites from termite mounds. They also shape sticks into "spears" for hunting small primates. Chimps are the only apes that regularly eat meat. The protein helps to fuel their big brains.

A chimpanzee slurps up termites from its "fishing" stick. It even frays the end of the stick so it will pick up more insects.

Under Threat

All the non-human great apes are endangered, and gorillas and orangutans are critically endangered. They have been affected by habitat destruction, hunting, and disease, and have also been removed from the wild for the illegal pet trade.

Today the mountain gorilla's range is limited to the Virunga Mountains and one national park in Uganda.

An orangutan's face is bare, though males have fleshy cheek pads. The rest of the body is covered in straggly orange hair.

Sensitive lips test fruits for ripeness. The orangutan also makes lip-smacking sounds to communicate.

BORNEAN ORANGUTAN

PONGO PYGMAEUS
"LITTLE PERSON OF THE FOREST"

Habitat: Rain forests; Borneo
Length: Male 1.4 m (4.6 ft); female 1.2 m (4 ft)
Weight: Male 85 kg (187 lb); female 37 kg (82 lb)
Diet: Fruit, shoots, leaves
Lifespan: Up to 45 years
Wild population: 55,000; Critically Endangered

DID YOU KNOW? Orangutans' powerful arms are one-and-a-half times longer than their legs. A male's armspan can be 2 m (7 ft) from fingertip to fingertip.

Monkeys and Lemurs

Every mandrill troop is led by one dominant male. His red and blue facial markings are brighter than those of the females.

Monkeys and prosimians (lemurs, lorises, and bushbabies) are primates, like the apes, so they climb well and have opposable thumbs that can pick up objects. They can be distinguished from the apes because they usually have tails. They also have smaller bodies and smaller brains.

Monkey Business

There are around 260 monkey species. The "New World" monkeys that live in the treetops of Central and South American forests have prehensile (gripping) tails. They include tamarins, squirrel monkeys, and marmosets. "Old World" monkeys live in Africa and Asia in forests, grasslands, scrubland, swamps, and even cities. They include baboons, macaques, and langurs.

A spectacled langur baby is born with orange fur. It turns dusky brown by the age of six months.

Madagascar's Stars

Lemurs live only on the island of Madagascar. There are more than 100 species, ranging from Madame Berthe's mouse lemur—the smallest primate at just 30 g (1.1 oz)—to the indri at 9.5 kg (21 lb). More than 90 percent of lemur species are under threat of extinction.

The endangered ring-tailed lemur lives in dry forests and bush in Madagascar.

The male mandrill is the largest monkey. It can be almost 1 m (3.3 ft) long and weigh up to 36 kg (79 lb). Mandrills live in rain forests and grassland in West Africa.

Mandrills communicate with scent, calls, and visual signs. This threat yawn shows off the male's sharp canines.

MANDRILL

MANDRILLUS SPHINX

Habitat: Forests, farmland, grasslands; W Africa
Length: Male 90 cm (35.4 in);
  female 70 cm (27.6 in)
Weight: Male 32 kg (70.5 lb);
  female 26 kg (57.3 lb)
Diet: Leaves, fruit, insects, small mammals
Lifespan: Up to 20 years
Wild population: Unknown; Vulnerable

DID YOU KNOW? The Barbary macaque is the only macaque species found outside Asia. It is also the only wild primate that lives in Europe.

Marsupials

Kangaroos, koalas, and their relatives are marsupials, or pouched mammals. Most mammal babies develop inside their mother's body, and many can walk or even run shortly after birth. Marsupial babies are born tiny, underdeveloped, and helpless. They crawl into their mother's pouch to carry on growing there.

Australian Life

There are a few marsupial species, such as the opossums, in North and South America. However, most live in Australia and New Guinea. They include kangaroos, koalas, wombats, wallabies, quokkas, and Tasmanian devils. Pouched mammals were the only kind of mammal in Australia until early settlers brought non-native dogs, mice, and rabbits.

The large nose sniffs out fresh eucalyptus leaves and scent markings left by other koalas.

The red kangaroo is the largest marsupial. This young male will grow almost as tall as a human, be able to leap 9 m (29.5 ft), and run at 70 km/h (44 mph).

The mother's pouch holds the baby koala, which is called a joey.

KOALA

PHASCOLARCTOS CINEREUS
"ASHY POUCHED BEAR"

Habitat: Forests, scrub; E Australia
Length: Male 75 cm (30 in); female 70 cm (28 in)
Weight: Male 9 kg (19.8 lb); female 7 kg (15.4 lb)
Diet: Eucalyptus leaves
Lifespan: Up to 20 years
Wild population: 75,000; Vulnerable

All Sorts of Diet

Kangaroos and wallabies eat any grass or leaves, while koalas feed mainly on eucalyptus. Insect-eating marsupials, such as bilbies, bandicoots, and numbats, have pointed snouts for winkling minibeasts out of bark or soil. The Tasmanian devil is the largest carnivorous marsupial.

The Tasmanian devil is the size of a small dog but it can take prey as large as a medium kangaroo.

Extremely thick, waterproof fur protects the koala against hot and cold temperatures.

DID YOU KNOW? The female Virginia opossum has the shortest pregnancy of any mammal—just 12 days.

41

Rodents

Found everywhere except Antarctica, rodents make up 40 percent of all mammals. There are around 1,500 species, including mice, rats, squirrels, beavers, and porcupines. Capybaras are the largest rodents. Guinea pigs, gerbils, and hamsters are all rodents too.

Like all rodents, the red squirrel has teeth that never stop growing. It sometimes gnaws on old deer antlers to get extra calcium for its teeth.

Food and Family

Rodents have sharp incisor teeth that keep growing throughout their lives. They can eat very hard food without their teeth wearing down. Some species eat and spoil human food and spread disease—brown rats, black rats, and house mice are all pests. Rodents can live solitary lives, like the dormouse, or stay in family groups, like the beaver. Ground squirrels and mole rats form huge colonies.

The black–tailed prairie dog is a kind of ground squirrel. One colony in Texas contained an estimated 400 million prairie dogs and covered an area of 64,000 sq km (25,000 sq miles).

Ready for Anything!

Rodents live in a variety of habitats. Lemmings survive average winter temperatures of −34°C (−30°F) in the Arctic tundra. Kangaroo rats and gerbils have adapted to life in the desert environments.

The water vole lives alongside rivers and streams all over Europe. It builds a waterside burrow.

EUROPEAN RED SQUIRREL	
SCIURUS VULGARIS "COMMON SQUIRREL"	**Habitat:** Forests; Europe, Asia **Length:** 38 cm (15 in) **Weight:** 600 g (1.3 lb) **Diet:** Seeds, nuts, fungi, berries **Lifespan:** Up to 20 years **Wild population:** Unknown; Vulnerable

DID YOU KNOW? Brown rats are the world's most common wild mammal. In Paris, France, there are four rats for every person.

The red squirrel has a great sense of smel . This helps it to sniff out the stores of nuts that it buries to survive the winter.

The bushy tail provides balance as the squirrel leaps from branch to branch. Flicking and waving the tail is also a way to communicate.

The busy front paws collect pine cones, hazelnuts, beech nuts, and berries. Squirrels also eat buds, fungi, birds' eggs, and sap.

Paler fur on the squirrel's belly blurs the outline of its body, and makes it more difficult for predators to see.

Wild Pigs

Wild pigs are intelligent and adaptable hoofed mammals native to Europe, Africa, and Asia, and introduced to Australia and the Americas. They include wild boar, peccaries, warthogs, and bush pigs. Wild pigs have stocky bodies, short legs, and long snouts with large nostrils.

Pigs have a good sense of smell that can detect food even buried underground. They use their snout to dig, touch, and feel.

Wild Pig Diet

Pigs are omnivores. They forage for roots, bulbs, nuts, berries, and seeds. They also eat worms, beetle grubs, birds' eggs, small mammals, reptiles, and amphibians. The warthog is the only wild pig that eats grass. It lives on the African savannah.

Wild boar piglets have striped coats that help them to blend in with the leaf litter. The stripes start to fade at about three months.

The warthog is named for the warty lumps on its head. Its long upper teeth, or tusks, can grow 30 cm (12 in) long.

WILD BOAR

SUS SCROFA "DIGGING PIG"

Habitat: Forests, farmland, grasslands; Europe, Asia, N Africa
Length: Male 1.7 m (5.6 ft); female 1.3 m (4.3 ft)
Weight: Male 190 kg (419 lb); female 135 kg (298 lb)
Diet: Plants, insects, eggs, small animals
Lifespan: Up to 14 years
Wild population: Unknown; Least Concern

DID YOU KNOW? There are around one billion domestic pigs around the world today. They are all descended from the wild boar.

Wild boars live in groups called sounders, made up of sows and their piglets. Sounders usually contain about 20 animals.

Pigs are short–sighted. They cannot see detail from a distance but they are good at spotting movement.

Terrific Tusks

Male wild pigs have enlarged canine teeth called tusks that continue growing throughout their life. The babirusa's upward-curving tusks pierce through its snout and will eventually cut into its skull if it does not wear them down regularly.

The babirusa lives near rivers in Indonesian rain forests. Only the male has the huge, curved tusks.

45

Chapter Three

Birds

Birds are warm-blooded animals with feathers, whose front limbs have evolved into wings. They have toothless, beaked jaws and their young hatch from eggs. There are nearly 11,000 species of bird. They communicate with each other using songs and calls, and some are amazing mimics.

High Flyers

Some birds, such as penguins, have lost the power of flight but many fly extraordinary distances. Some birds are so well adapted to flight that they rarely land. The wandering albatross can stay on the wing for distances up to 16,090 km (10,000 miles).

The wandering albatross has the widest wingspan of any bird—up to 3.5 m (11.5 ft) across.

HOATZIN

OPISTHOCOMUS HOAZIN

"PHEASANT WITH LONG HAIR BEHIND"

Habitat: Swamps, forests; S America
Length: 65 cm (25.6 in)
Wingspan: 50 cm (20 in)
Weight: 800 g (1.8 lb)
Diet: Leaves, fruit, flowers
Lifespan: Up to 10 years
Wild population: Unknown; Least concern

DID YOU KNOW? The Arctic tern makes the longest migration. Each year it flies up to 90,000 km (56,000 miles) from the Arctic to Antarctica and back again.

Eggs and Nests

Birds reproduce by laying hard-shelled eggs that need to be incubated (kept at a warm, steady temperature). Most birds sit on their eggs and use their own body heat to keep them warm. When the eggs hatch, most chicks are helpless. They rely on their parents to bring them food.

Birds evolved from theropods, carnivorous dinosaurs that walked on two legs. Their feathers developed from scales.

Blackbird chicks open their beaks for food from their father. Only the female blackbird incubates the eggs, but both parents feed the chicks.

Owls

Owls are raptors, or hunting birds, found almost everywhere except the Antarctic. There are around 200 species, ranging from the tiny, insect-eating elf owl to the Eurasian eagle owl that takes prey as large as deer. Owls are solitary birds and most of them are active only at night.

The enormous eyes let in as much light as possible when the owl is hunting at night. They are also very sensitive to movement.

Super Senses

Owls have huge, forward-facing eyes and can swivel their head 270 degrees to gain good all-round vision. Owls also have excellent hearing. They fly so silently that they can hear the faint rustlings of small mammals down on the ground.

Strong feet with sharp talons can catch and kill small animals. The bottom of each foot has rough, knobbly skin that gives extra grip on struggling prey.

The long-eared owl is named for the feathered tufts on its head, but these are not actually ears. They are just there to make the owl look bigger.

BARN OWL
TYTO ALBA
"WHITE OWL"

Habitat: Grasslands, farmland, scrub; Almost worldwide
Length: 37 cm (1.2 ft)
Wingspan: Male 90 cm (3 ft); female 105 cm (3.4 ft)
Weight: Male 470 g (1 lb); female 570 g (1.3 lb)
Diet: Small mammals, amphibians, lizards, insects
Lifespan: Up to 5 years
Wild population: Unknown; Least Concern

No Place Like Home

Owls are one of the few birds that don't make their own nest. They reuse other birds' old nests or lay their eggs in a hollow tree. Some owls bring up their chicks in the rafters of a barn. Others find a rocky ledge, a hollow in the ground, or even a burrow.

Eastern screech owls use any natural or artificial cavity as a nesting site. These chicks are being raised in a nestbox.

The super-soft feathers make almost no noise in flight because fringed wing edges muffle any sound. The owl flies silently.

Hidden beneath feathers are sensitive ears that can detect a mouse moving through grass from a distance of 10 m (33 ft).

DID YOU KNOW? The largest owl, Blakiston's eagle owl, has a 2-m (6.6-ft) wingspan. It lives in Russia, China, and Japan but is endangered.

Vultures

Vultures are the vacuum cleaners of the natural world. They eat carrion (dead bodies). Without vultures, the decaying bodies of dead animals would spread disease. Rotting meat contains deadly microbes, but vultures have extremely strong stomach acid that kills these.

The powerful beak can rip through skin and flesh, and pull off chunks of meat.

The bald head and neck won't get clogged up with blood while feasting—feathers would!

Seek and Find

Although vultures are meat eaters, they rarely kill prey. They prefer to scavenge. They glide high on warm air currents, seeking out carrion with their excellent senses of smell and sight. They watch each other carefully—if one drops to earth, the others quickly follow.

A large carcass can attract as many as 100 vultures from eight different species. The biggest birds feed first, because they have the strength to tear open the body.

KING VULTURE

SARCORAMPHUS PAPA
"FLESH BEAK FATHER"

Habitat: Forests, grasslands, swamps; C & S America
Length: 75 cm (2.5 ft)
Wingspan: 1.8 m (5.9 ft)
Weight: 4 kg (8.8 lb)
Diet: Carrion
Lifespan: Up to 25 years
Wild population: Unknown; Least Concern

DID YOU KNOW? The Ruppell's griffon vulture is the highest-flying bird. One was recorded at 11,277 m (37,000 ft)—the altitude at which jets fly.

The folds of loose skin on the head are called lappets.

The king vulture is the showiest member of the vulture family. The skin around its neck can be orange, red, yellow, or purple.

The California condor is North America's largest bird, with a wingspan of up to 3.4 m (11 ft).

Back from the Brink

The California condor became extinct in the wild in 1987 because of habitat loss, poaching, and lead poisoning. Thanks to a breeding programme, it has been reintroduced to parts of Arizona and Utah, but it is still one of the world's rarest birds.

Eagles

Eagles are the largest raptors, or birds of prey. They have large, powerful bodies, broad wings, hooked beaks, sharp talons, and keen sight. There are over 60 species. They hunt during the day in a range of habitats—mountains, forests, deserts, grasslands, marshes, and coasts.

Eagle-Eyed

Eagles probably have the best eyesight in the animal world. Their eyes work like telescopes to magnify distant objects, and are particularly good at spotting movement. An eagle flying 300 m (1,000 ft) above the ground can see a mammal moving 3.2 km (2 miles) away. They even see fish in water.

The sharp, hooked beak is designed to pull away fur or feathers and tear flesh into chunks.

Excellent eyesight helps the bald eagle to spot fish in lakes or the sea. On average, fish makes up more than half of a bald eagle's diet.

These white-tailed eagles are locking talons. Eagles fight in mid-air over food or, sometimes, for the right to mate with a female.

DID YOU KNOW? The Philippine eagle is the world's rarest eagle. There are fewer than 250 breeding pairs left in the wild, and they are critically endangered.

Partners

Nomadic peoples in Central Asia have been catching and training eagles to help them to hunt for at least 6,000 years. Kazakh people in Mongolia's Altai Mountains use golden eagles to hunt foxes and hares. Kazakh children start working with a bird from the age of 12.

The partnership between a Kazakh hunter and his eagle can last 30 years or more.

The eyes can see long-distance detail. They can also detect ultraviolet light, which is invisible to the human eye.

The powerful flight muscles make up more than a third of the bird's body weight. The white-tailed eagle has one of the greatest wingspans of any eagle.

WHITE-TAILED EAGLE

HALIAEETUS ALBICILLA

Habitat: Lakes, coastal areas; N Europe, N Asia
Length: Male 80 cm (2.6 ft); female 92 cm (3 ft)
Wingspan: Male 2.2 m (7.2 ft); female 2.4 m (7.9 ft)
Weight: Male 5.5 kg (12 lb); female 6 kg (13.2 lb)
Diet: Mammals, birds, fish
Lifespan: Up to 36 years
Wild population: 40,000; Least Concern

Showing Off

Some birds advertise for a mate or announce their ownership of a territory with complicated songs. Others signal with vibrant feathers and displays that rivals can easily see. Bird feathers are some of the most eye-catching objects in the animal world.

Forest Feathers

Many rain forest-dwelling birds rely on dazzling plumage to find a mate in the gloom of the jungle. From birds-of-paradise to parrots, these birds have showy feathers in a rainbow of hues. Toucans draw attention to themselves with a different feature—their large, bright bill!

The peacock's heavy train (tail) makes up more than 60 percent of its body weight. The healthiest, fittest males have the biggest, flashiest trains.

The Indian peafowl is native to forests in South Asia. Prized for the male's spectacular plumage, it has been introduced to parks and other habitats all over the world.

The toco toucan lives in South America. Its enormous orange bill is up to 23 cm (9.1 in) long—that's a third of the bird's body length.

INDIAN PEAFOWL

PAVO CRISTATUS
"CRESTED PEAFOWL"

Habitat: Forests, farmland, grassland; S Asia
Length: Male 2.1 m (6.9 ft); female 0.95 m (3.1 ft)
Wingspan: Male 1.5 m (4.9 ft); female 1.2 m (3.9 ft)
Weight: Male 5.5 kg (12.1 lb); female 3.5 kg (7.7 lb)
Diet: Insects, seeds, fruit, reptiles, small mammals
Lifespan: Up to 30 years
Wild population: Unknown; Least Concern

DID YOU KNOW? Only the peacock has bright feathers, not the peahen. Like many female birds, she is a dull brown. It makes her harder to spot when sitting on her eggs.

Each tail feather ends with a striking eyespot. The bird shakes and rattles the fanned-out train for added effect.

Courtship

The male bowerbird wins the prize for the most extraordinary courtship display. First it builds an arched structure called a bower from dried grasses. Then it collects and arranges beautiful objects in front of the bower. Female birds tour several bowers before they decide on a mate.

A male satin bowerbird displays feathers, petals, shells, wrappers, and bottle tops in front of its bower—anything as long as it is blue!

The highlights on the iridescent green feathers shift from silver to blue, depending on the light.

Parrots

There are nearly 400 species of parrot. The pygmy parrot is the smallest at just 8 cm (3.1 in) long. The hyacinth macaw is the biggest at 1 m (3.3 ft). Parrots are some of the world's most intelligent birds and a few have even learned to use tools.

Bright red, yellow, and blue feathers help a scarlet macaw spot other scarlet macaws in the forest.

No two macaws have the same feather patterns and shades. They are all different.

Feet act like hands, lifting food to the parrot's mouth.

DID YOU KNOW? The kakapo is a flightless parrot that lives in New Zealand. It is critically endangered, but its population is rising from around 60 in 1999 to more than 160 today.

The strong, sharp beak can crack tough nut shells, and hold on to branches when climbing.

Life in the Canopy

Parrots spend most of their lives in the treetops, searching for food and keeping away from predators on the forest floor. They are noisy birds that use their loud, screeching voices to keep in contact with other members of their flock. They usually nest in tree holes, high above the ground.

Rainbow lorikeets are medium-sized parrots, native to Australia's tropical forests. They feed on fruit, pollen, and nectar.

Parrot Evolution

Parrots first appeared around 60 million years ago. Early species were meat eaters but now parrots feed on nuts and other seeds, buds, flowers, and fruit. Occasionally they eat insects. Unfortunately some species are endangered because of habitat loss and the pet trade.

Every year thousands of parrots are caught in the wild and sold as pets.

SCARLET MACAW

ARA MACAO

Habitat: Rain forests; C & S America
Length: 90 cm (2.9 ft)
Wingspan: 1 m (3.3 ft)
Weight: 1 kg (2.2 lb)
Diet: Nuts, seeds, fruit
Lifespan: Up to 50 years
Wild population: Unknown; Vulnerable

Hummingbirds

There are around 325 hummingbird species, all native to the Americas. These amazing little birds take their name from the humming sound of their fast-beating wings, which can flap up to 200 times a second. Hummingbirds have one of the highest heart rates of any animal—an average of 1,200 beats per minute.

The rufous hummingbird winters in Mexico and heads to its breeding grounds in Canada and Alaska in spring. It is found farther north than any other hummingbird.

The male rufous hummingbird has an iridescent orange–red throat patch.

The wings have a total span of just 11 cm (4.3 in), but carry the rufous hummingbird on a 3,200-km (2,000-mile) migration twice a year.

Aerial Acrobatics

Hummingbirds are the only bird that can fly upside down and backward. Their top flight speed is 48 km/h (30 mph). Adaptations that make them more lightweight include fewer feathers and smaller feet. Their feet and legs are not strong enough to walk on.

The wings of a hovering hummingbird, such as this male golden–tailed sapphire hummingbird, move almost too fast to see.

RUFOUS HUMMINGBIRD

SELASPHORUS RUFUS
"REDDISH LIGHT CARRIER"

Habitat: Scrub, parks, gardens, woodlands, swamps, meadows; N & C America
Length: 8 cm (3.1 in)
Wingspan: 11 cm (4.3 in)
Weight: 4 g (0.1 oz)
Diet: Nectar, insects
Lifespan: Up to 5 years
Wild population: Unknown; Least Concern

The long, thin beak is designed to probe flowers and snap up insects. It houses a long tongue that darts in and out up to 20 times a second as it slurps up nectar.

Constant Snacking

All hummingbirds eat nectar and pollen. They hover in front of a flower and lick out the nectar with their long, grooved tongue. A hummingbird can visit 2,000 flowers in a day and consume twice its own body weight. They also catch and eat tiny insects while on the wing.

A sword–billed hummingbird and two speckled hummingbirds take nectar from an artificial feeder.

DID YOU KNOW? The bee hummingbird is the world's smallest bird. It weighs just 1.8 g (0.06 oz)—about the same as a paperclip.

Penguins

Penguins lost the ability to fly more than 60 million years ago, and their wings have evolved into stiff, strong flippers. These birds can be clumsy on land but they are graceful in water, where they zoom after fish, squid, and krill. Almost all 17 penguin species live in the southern hemisphere.

Homelands

Most penguins inhabit temperate zones. Galápagos penguins live farthest north, just above the equator. Only two penguin species (the Adélie and emperor) live in Antarctica, but chinstrap, gentoo, and macaroni penguins breed there.

The emperor penguin is the largest penguin, standing up to 1.2 m (4 ft) tall. Breeding colonies in Antarctica can contain thousands of birds.

Feeding Challenges

Penguins dive after food but surface regularly to breathe air. Emperor penguins are the champion divers, reaching depths of 535 m (1,755 ft). Once prey is caught by the penguin, it cannot escape—it is snared on the backward-pointing spines that line the bird's mouth.

The rockhopper is one of the smallest penguins. It dives down 100 m (330 ft) to hunt fish, crustaceans, squid, and krill.

Like all penguins, king penguins appear to "fly" underwater. This species has golden feathers around its neck and head.

The short tail helps the penguin to balance when it is waddling on land.

Eyes can work in water or in air.

Closely packed feathers keep cold water away from the skin. The feathers also trap air, helping the penguin to float in water.

The streamlined flippers are covered in short, sleek feathers. Long ones would drag in the water.

KING PENGUIN

APTENODYTES PATAGONICUS

"WINGLESS DIVER FROM PATAGONIA"

Habitat: Cold oceans, islands; Antarctica
Height: Male 95 cm (3.1 ft);
   female 85 cm (2.8 ft)
Weight: Male 12.5 kg (27.6 lb);
   female 11.1 kg (24.5 lb)
Diet: Fish, squid
Lifespan: Up to 20 years
Wild population: 2.2 million; Least Concern

DID YOU KNOW? A male emperor penguin spends 70 days balancing its egg snugly on its feet in Antarctica, where winter temperatures drop as low as −50°C (−58°F).

Water Birds

Flamingos spend most of their time wading, but they are also good fliers. Some species migrate.

Many birds have adapted to live in or around water. They include gulls, penguins, and other seabirds, as well as shoreline birds such as pelicans, curlews, and sandpipers. Wetlands are home to herons, ibises, storks, flamingos, and cranes. Ducks and geese are also water birds.

Fresh- and Saltwater

There are nearly 150 species of ducks, geese, and swans, and they are all closely related. Most live in freshwater habitats, but some ducks can cope with life at sea. Sea ducks feed on fish and only visit land to nest. Freshwater ducks eat plants and invertebrates. They rest and graze on land.

The harlequin duck is a small sea duck. It dives down to catch shellfish.

Tough, scaly skin on flamingos' legs lets them live in toxically salty lakes.

Seabird Cities

Most seabirds nest in huge groups called colonies. Hundreds or thousands of birds cram into crevices or on clifftops, returning to the same site year after year. The colony is noisy and smelly, but also safe. Being part of a big group makes the birds, their eggs, and their chicks less vulnerable to predators.

Puffins nest in rocky crevices or shallow burrows. They can stick with the same partner for 20 years.

Flamingos are filter-feeders. They suck in water, and hair-like filters in the beak trap shrimps, algae, and other food.

Hundreds of thousands of lesser flamingos feed and breed at Lake Bogoria in Kenya. The super-salty water puts off predators.

LESSER FLAMINGO

PHOENICONAIAS MINOR
"SMALL CRIMSON FEATHER"

Habitat: Lakes, coastal areas; Africa, India
Height: 85 cm (2.8 ft)
Wingspan: 1 m (3.3 ft)
Weight: 2.5 kg (5.5 lb)
Diet: Algae, insects, small crustaceans
Lifespan: Up to 35 years
Wild population: Unknown; Near Threatened

DID YOU KNOW? Flamingos hatch with charcoal feathers. They turn pink because of a natural dye in their diet of shrimps and blue-green algae.

Flightless Giants

Ratites are large birds with a breastbone that cannot support flight wings. Ostriches, emus, cassowaries, and rheas are all ratites. Extinct giant birds such as the moa and elephant bird were ratites too.

For most of the year, the ostrich lives alone or in a pair with chicks. In the breeding season, ostriches gather in large flocks.

Global Family

The ostrich is the world's tallest and heaviest bird. South America's flightless giant is the rhea. Australia is home to the emu and New Guinea has the cassowary. The kiwi is a rare, duck-sized ratite that lives in New Zealand.

The cassowary can swallow large rain forest fruits whole, thanks to its stretchy neck.

The 5 cm/2 in-wide eyes are larger than any other land animal's. They are fringed with lashes that shade them from the sun.

OSTRICH

STRUTHIO CAMELUS
"CAMEL SPARROW"

Habitat: Grasslands, farmland, semi-desert; sub-Saharan Africa
Height: Male 2.6 m (8.5 ft); female 1.9 m (6.2 ft)
Wingspan: Male 2 m (6.6 ft); female 1.9 m (6.2 ft)
Weight: Male 115 kg (254 lb); female 100 kg (220 lb)
Diet: Seeds, grass, insects, fruit, leaves
Lifespan: Up to 40 years
Wild population: Unknown; Least Concern

Soft, fluffy feathers—black for males and brown for females—keep the bird warm on cold nights. The wings span 2 m (6.5 ft) and are stuck out for balance when the bird runs.

Featherless legs help the ostrich to lose body heat and keep its temperature steady. Powerful muscles let it outrun most predators.

Ground Nests

Ratites nest on the ground, but that leaves the eggs and young vulnerable. The eggs are protected by super-tough shells. Chicks can run and even swim as soon as they hatch. If a predator approaches an ostrich family, the male tries to lure it away while the young run to safety with their mother.

The two toes on each foot (most birds have three or four) provide great grip. They can also deliver killer kicks if the ostrich faces a predator.

A rhea nest holds dozens of eggs. The male incubates the eggs, all laid by different females he has mated with, and he also raises the chicks.

DID YOU KNOW? A sprinting ostrich takes 3.6-m (12-ft) strides and reaches 70 km/h (43 mph). It's the fastest animal on two legs!

Chapter Four
Reptiles and Amphibians

Reptiles and amphibians are both animal groups that are vertebrates (have backbones) and cannot make their own body heat (are "cold-blooded" or ectothermic). Reptiles include lizards, alligators, crocodiles, turtles, and snakes. Amphibians include frogs, toads, and salamanders.

Water and Land

Amphibians spend their early life in water, breathing through gills, then develop lungs and live on land. Their name means "two lives." Amphibian skin is thin, but reptiles have scaly, watertight skin. Most reptiles live on land and they all use lungs to breathe air—even sea turtles. "Reptile" comes from the Latin word for "crawling."

Metamorphosis

Almost all amphibians undergo a change, or metamorphosis. With its gills and fishy tail, a tadpole looks nothing like its parents. At five weeks its back legs sprout and by ten weeks, the froglet has front legs and a shorter tail. By 14 weeks, it looks like a tiny frog.

The caecilian is a strange, worm-like amphibian. Most species live underground. They use their needle-sharp teeth to eat worms, termites, and even snakes, frogs, and lizards.

Frog larvae (young) are called tadpoles. They do not have legs yet but they have a tail that helps them to swim.

A few reptiles give birth to live young, but most lay eggs. The eggs are soft, like thick paper. This hatchling is a green iguana.

GREEN IGUANA

IGUANA IGUANA

Habitat: Forests; C & S America
Length: Male 1.8 m (5.9ft);
  female 1.5 m (4.9 ft)
Weight: Male 4 kg (9 lb);
  female 3 kg (6.6 lb)
Diet: Leaves, flowers, fruit
Lifespan: Up to 20 years
Wild population: Unknown; Least Concern

DID YOU KNOW? A female frog can produce 20,000 eggs
a year. Only one in 100 survives to be an adult frog.

Venomous Snakes

Some snakes paralyze or kill their prey by injecting it with venom. Venomous snakes include cobras, vipers, rattlesnakes, and death adders. They are smaller than constrictors (snakes that kill by squeezing), but they can move fast. The black mamba hits 20 km/h (12 mph)!

Deadly Killers

Australia is home to some of the world's most venomous snakes: tiger snakes, taipans, and brown snakes. Other deadly species include kraits, sea kraits, and sea snakes. Sea snakes inhabit warm, tropical oceans. They breathe air but spend their lives in water.

The banded sea krait's black and yellow stripes warn that it is extremely venomous.

Many vipers have heat-sensing pits that detect prey's body heat. Bush vipers do not have these pits.

BUSH VIPER

ATHERIS SQUAMIGERA

Habitat: Forests; Central Africa
Length: Male 65 cm (25.6 in); female 70 cm (27.6 in)
Weight: Male 400 g (0.9 lb); female 650 g (1.4 lb)
Diet: Birds, reptiles, rodents, amphibians
Lifespan: Up to 20 years
Wild population: Unknown; Vulnerable

Defensive Technique

There are 14 spitting cobra species—seven in Africa and seven in Asia. These unusual snakes can squirt venom at predators or prey. Sprayed from holes in the fangs, the venom travels as far as 2 m (6.6 ft). It is usually fired at the victim's eyes to cause temporary blindness.

Venom drips from a red spitting cobra's fangs. This snake lives in East Africa.

Sight is the bush viper's most important sense. The snake uses body language to communicate.

The bush viper's rough, overlapping scales can be yellow, green, olive, brown, black, red, or orange.

DID YOU KNOW? The inland taipan has the most dangerous venom of any reptile. A single bite contains enough toxins to kill 100 people in less than 45 minutes.

69

Constrictors

Like most snake species, female green tree pythons are slightly larger than the males.

Constrictors live in the tropics and include boas, pythons, and anacondas. These snakes do not kill their prey with venom. Instead, they coil around their victim's body and squeeze tightly until its blood stops flowing. This cuts off vital oxygen from the heart and brain and the prey quickly dies.

Slow Food

Most snakes are ambush predators that lie in wait rather than actively hunt. They digest their food slowly and may not eat again for months after a big meal. Being cold-blooded, snakes do not use up energy making their own body heat. They spend most of their time resting.

Mature, heavy boa constrictors hide among the leaves on the rain forest floor. Younger ones ambush their prey from trees.

The green tree python only turns green when it is about a year old. It is born bright yellow, orange, or red.

GREEN TREE PYTHON

MORELIA VIRIDIS
"GREEN PYTHON"

Habitat: Rain forests, scrub; SE Asia, N Australia
Length: Male 1.5 m (4.9 ft); female 2 m (6.6 ft)
Weight: Male 1.1 kg (2.4 lb); female 1.6 kg (3.5 lb)
Diet: Small mammals, reptiles
Lifespan: Up to 20 years
Wild population: Unknown; Least Concern

DID YOU KNOW? The world's longest snake is the reticulated python of Southeast Asia. It can grow up to 9 m (30 ft) long.

The python bites its prey before constriction, but its saliva contains no venom.

A resting tree python coils its body over a branch and places its head in the middle.

Big Meals

Snakes' teeth are for gripping food, not for chewing. They swallow prey headfirst and whole. Snakes' jaws have elastic ligaments so they can stretch really wide. Anacondas—the world's heaviest snakes—take the largest prey animals. They catch and eat deer and even jaguars.

Anacondas lurk in swamps and lakes with just their eyes above the water. This one is swallowing an iguana.

Frogs

Frogs are by far the most common kind of amphibian—there are around 4,800 different species. They range in size from a tiny 7-mm (0.3-in) frog that lives on the floor of Papua New Guinea's rain forests (and holds the record for smallest vertebrate) to Africa's well-named 32-cm (12.6-in) goliath frog.

Frogs on the Move

Most frogs are strong swimmers and exceptional jumpers. Their legs have stretchy muscles that are pulled in when the frog is at rest. If an enemy approaches, the legs kick back and the muscles act as a spring to push the frog through the air.

The frog has a large, sensitive ear behind each eye. It has keen hearing.

The tree frog has sticky pads at the end of its fingers and toes for extra grip.

Frogs jump horizontally rather than up into the air. Many species can leap more than 20 times their own body length.

DID YOU KNOW? Puerto Rico's common coqui frog is the world's noisiest amphibian. Males are just 3.4 cm (1.3 in) long, but their calls hit 100 decibels.

A frog blinks when it swallows its food. This pushes its eyes into the head, forcing the struggling insect down the frog's throat.

Skin Deep

Poison dart frogs live in Central and South American rain forests and come in eye-catching blues, reds, greens, oranges, yellows, and blacks. Their bright skin is a warning to predators that it tastes bad and contains toxic chemicals. The most poisonous, the golden poison frog, contains enough toxin to kill up to 20 people.

Bulging eyes can see about 280 degrees all around. This is useful because the frog cannot bend its neck.

Poison dart frogs are tiny. The largest species, this dyeing dart frog, is just 5 cm (2 in) long.

RED-EYED TREE FROG

AGALYCHNIS CALLIDRYAS
"BEAUTIFUL SHINING TREE NYMPH"

Habitat: Rain forests; C America
Length: Male 5 cm (2 in);
  female 7.5 cm (3 in)
Weight: Male 10 g (0.3 oz);
  female 15 g (0.5 oz)
Diet: Small insects, other invertebrates
Lifespan: Up to 5 years
Wild population: Unknown; Least Concern

Toads

Toads are frogs that have dry skin with warty bumps, instead of the usual moist, smooth skin. They can live farther away from water than other frogs. Toads also move differently—crawling, rather than hopping—and do not have such bulging eyes. The smallest toad is North America's 3.3-cm (1.3-in) oak toad.

Croak Chorus

Like all frogs, toads must lay their eggs in water. In the breeding season males travel to lakes, ponds, and rivers. They advertise for mates with croaky calls, amplified by an inflatable sac of skin beneath the throat. The croaking attracts nearby females. Big pools can contain hundreds of male toads that croak all night long.

The guttural toad is named for the male's call (guttural means "throaty" or "harsh-sounding"). It is common across sub-Saharan Africa.

CANE TOAD

RHINELLA MARINA
"SMALL-NOSED FROM THE SEA"

Habitat: Grasslands, farmland, scrub; C & S America, Australia
Length: Male 14 cm (5.5 in); female 20 cm (7.9 in)
Weight: Male 550 g (1.2 lb); female 900 g (2 lb)
Diet: Rodents, reptiles, amphibians, invertebrates
Lifespan: Up to 15 years
Wild population: Unknown; Least Concern

The large poison gland on the shoulder produces bufotenin, a toxin that is fatal to many animals.

Eggs, Tadpoles, and Toadlets

The female toad lays thousands of eggs in long strings that wind around plants at the margins of the pool. The tadpoles hatch after a week or two and stay in the water for four to six weeks. By then they have metamorphosed (changed) into toadlets that can survive on land.

The male midwife toad wraps strings of fertilized eggs around his back legs to keep them safe. When they are about to hatch, he takes them to a pool.

Native to the Americas, the cane toad was introduced to Australia and other places to control sugarcane beetles. Unfortunately it is now a threat to local wildlife.

The cane toad has dry, warty skin. Its back toes are partly webbed, but the front ones are not.

DID YOU KNOW? The female cane toad lays up to 25,000 eggs at once. Each string can be up to 20 m (66 ft) long.

Salamanders

Salamanders have slim, lizard-shaped bodies with short legs and long tails, but they are not reptiles—they are amphibians, like frogs. They can survive on land or in water. There are more than 500 species, including newts. Salamanders are the only vertebrates that can regrow a lost leg.

Scary Skin

Their showy skin warns predators that salamanders taste unpleasant and are toxic. All species ooze some kind of toxin from their skin and some are highly poisonous. The rough-skinned newt, which lives in North America, contains a poison called tetrodotoxin that can be fatal to humans.

A slender body is the perfect shape for spending the day hidden under a rock, log, or pile of leaves.

The fire salamander is named for its markings, which resemble flickering yellow or orange flames.

The poison glands on the emperor newt's back look like orange warts. They contain enough toxins to kill 7,500 mice!

Roughened skin on the toes gives the salamander a better grip on slippy rocks or leaves. Some newts have webbed back feet.

The fire salamander flicks out its tongue to catch worms, slugs, spiders, and insects.

FIRE SALAMANDER

SALAMANDRA SALAMANDRA

Habitat: Damp forests; Europe
Length: 20 cm (7.9 in)
Weight: 40 g (1.4 oz)
Diet: Worms, slugs, insects, other invertebrates
Lifespan: Up to 40 years
Wild population: Unknown; Least Concern

Long, flat tail moves from side to side when the salamander swims or runs.

Forever Young

Most amphibians spend their larval stage in water and then lose their gills to live on land as adults. The axolotl never loses its gills. This salamander, which is native to Mexico, stays in water all its life. The axolotl is critically endangered because of habitat loss and pollution.

The axolotl has three pairs of feathery gills. It uses them to collect oxygen from the water.

DID YOU KNOW? The Chinese giant salamander is the world's largest amphibian. It can be up to 1.8 m (5.9 ft) long and weigh 50 kg (110 lb).

Turtles

Turtles make up a family called chelonians—reptiles that have a protective shell of bone or cartilage. Ones that live in water have flippers for swimming. Turtles that live on land, often known as tortoises, have four short, powerful legs. Like all reptiles, chelonians cannot make their own body heat.

Tiny magnetic crystals in the turtle's brain let it use Earth's magnetic field to navigate.

Landlubbers

Tortoises range in size from the Cape speckled tortoise at around 100 g (3.5 oz) to the Galápagos giant tortoise at more than 400 kg (880 lb). They live in deserts, semi-arid zones, swamps, and rain forests. They dig deep burrows to avoid extreme temperatures.

The ornate box turtle lives in the semi-arid prairies of the American Midwest.

Coming up for Air

Sea turtles usually surface to breathe every five to 40 minutes, but can stay underwater for hours when they are sleeping. Freshwater turtles take a breath every half-hour. Some species, such as the alligator snapping turtle, hibernate through the winter at the bottom of a pond. They hold their breath for months!

The alligator snapping turtle has a worm-like lure in its mouth that tempts fish to approach.

GREEN SEA TURTLE

CHELONIA MYDAS
"WET TORTOISE"

Habitat: Warm oceans; near the equator
Length: 1.3 m (4.3 ft);
Weight: 150 kg (331 lb)
Diet: Young: jellyfish, marine invertebrates, crustaceans; adults: sea grass, algae
Lifespan: Up to 80 years
Wild population: Unknown; Endangered

Hard shell of modified bone is covered with plates of keratin (the stuff that makes our nails). It protects the turtle's organs.

The green sea turtle is the second-largest of the seven sea turtle species, after the leatherback.

The turtle cannot pull its flippers or its head into its shell.

Paddle–like front flippers power the turtle along. Some green sea turtles migrate 2,094 km (1,300 miles) from their nesting grounds to their feeding grounds.

DID YOU KNOW? Tortoises live longer than any other land animal. An Aldabra giant tortoise called Adwaita was a record 255 years old when he died in Kolkata Zoo, India, in 2006.

Chameleons

Chameleons are very specialized lizards that mostly live in trees. There are more than 200 species, of which almost half are found only on the island of Madagascar. Chameleons are famous for being great masters of disguise, but not all species have the special cells that let them change the appearance of their skin.

Unique Eyes

Chameleons are the only animals with two eyes that work independently. One can look forward, while the other looks back, and each eye swivels in all directions. All-round vision helps chameleons to pinpoint the position of fast-moving prey. Most chameleons feed on insects. Larger species, such as Parson's chameleon, also take lizards and birds.

A chameleon catches an insect on its sticky, elastic tongue. The tongue catapults out and back into the mouth too fast for the human eye to see!

DID YOU KNOW? The world's smallest chameleon is a species of leaf chameleon called *Brookesia micra*. Discovered on Madagascar in 2012, it is less than 3 cm (1.1 in) long.

Chameleons can pick up vibrations but do not have an external ear. Sight is a much more important sense for them.

Quick Change

Chameleons communicate with each other by turning from green to blue, yellow, red, brown, white, or black. They also change in response to the temperature. Turning black can be a sign of nervousness, while yellow can mean the chameleon wants to be left alone.

Green skin indicates to other chameleons that this female veiled chameleon is feeling calm.

Most chameleons have a prehensile tail that acts like a fifth limb. The tail can hold onto branches when the chameleon climbs.

Two toes on one side of the branch and three on the other give the chameleon a secure grip.

PARSON'S CHAMELEON

CHAMAELEO PARSONII

Habitat: Forests; Madagascar
Length: 60 cm (2 ft)
Weight: 700 g (1.5 lb)
Diet: Insects, other invertebrates
Lifespan: Up to 7 years
Wild population: Unknown; Near Endangered

Lizards

There are more than 6,000 lizard species worldwide (except in very cold habitats). They include iguanas, monitors, geckos, anoles, skinks, and chameleons. Lizards are reptiles that usually have four legs, clawed feet, and a long tail, but there are some legless species.

Dish of the Day

Lizards are varied, and so are their diets. Smaller kinds, such as geckos, feed on crickets, flies, and other insects. Larger ones, such as frilled lizards, also eat small reptiles and mammals. Marine iguanas, the only seagoing lizards, graze on seaweed. The terrifying Komodo dragon kills deer and pigs and also eats carrion.

Glands on the marine iguana's head get rid of all the sea salt it takes in with its food. The short snout and sharp, tiny teeth are perfect for grazing on seaweed and other algae.

Native to rain forests in Southeast Asia, the Tokay gecko also enters people's homes. It hunts cockroaches and other invertebrates.

MARINE IGUANA

AMBLYRHYNCHUS CRISTATUS "CRESTED BLUNT SNOUT"

Habitat: Coastal areas; Galápagos Islands
Length: Male 70–120 cm (2.3–4 ft); female 60–100 cm (2–3.3 ft)
Weight: Male 1–13 kg (2.2–29 lb); female 0.5–9 kg (1.1–20 lb)
Diet: Marine algae
Lifespan: Up to 12 years
Wild population: Unknown; Vulnerable

DID YOU KNOW? The Komodo dragon, a kind of monitor, is the world's largest lizard. It can reach 3 m (9.8 ft) long and weigh up to 70 kg (154 lb). It also has a venomous bite.

Defensive Strategies

The frilled lizard scares off predators by unfurling its neck frill and hissing, while the horned lizard's technique is to squirt blood from its eyes! Most lizards, however, run from danger. Many species drop their tail—its violent wriggling distracts the predator while the lizard escapes.

The armadillo lizard rolls into a ball if a predator approaches. It is protected by thick, spiny scales.

Red blotches can appear on the skin in summer. They are caused by pigments in certain seaweeds eaten by the lizard.

Crocodiles

Crocodilians are an ancient family of reptiles that appeared during the age of the dinosaurs. As well as crocodiles, they include alligators, caimans, and the gharial. Crocodilians live in and around water worldwide in warm habitats. They are fierce predators.

Man-Eaters

Large crocodilians will eat anything. The saltwater crocodile catches monkeys, deer, kangaroos, and other land animals as well as turtles, sea snakes, and sharks. It has the strongest bite of any animal. It even eats people. Crocodiles carry out hundreds of attacks on humans each year, many of them fatal.

Crocodiles are ambush predators. They may lie in wait for hours before prey comes near. Then they lunge.

Under Threat

The gharial is a critically endangered crocodilian that lives in Asia. There are only around 200 left in the wild. In the past these reptiles were hunted for their skins. Today, many of their river habitats have been dammed. The sand banks where gharials nest are being used by farmers to graze cattle.

The gharial's long, thin snout is too small and weak to take large prey. It has sharp, thin teeth for catching fish.

AMERICAN ALLIGATOR

ALLIGATOR MISSISSIPPIENSIS
"MISSISSIPPI LIZARD"

Habitat: Lakes, swamps; southern USA
Length: Male 3.4 m (11.2 ft);
female 2.6 m (8.5 ft)
Weight: Male 270 kg (595 lb);
female 120 kg (265 lb)
Diet: Fish, birds, turtles, mammals
Lifespan: Up to 50 years
Wild population: 5 million; Least Concern

The alligator's snout is wide, rounded, and black. A crocodile's is different—it is narrow, pointed, and olive-green.

The alligator's underside has smooth scales, but its back is covered with bony plates. These protect the alligator and help to disguise it as a floating log.

The alligator has about 80 teeth. When they wear out or break, new ones grow. Over its life an alligator might have 3,000 teeth.

DID YOU KNOW? Crocodile hatchlings can only be male if the eggs were kept at around 32°C (89.6°F). Lower or higher temperatures produce females.

Chapter Five

Sea Creatures

Water covers more than two-thirds of our planet and the oceans are home to more life than the land. From tiny plankton to the colossal blue whale, animals have adapted to every marine environment. The 200 m (650 ft) closest to the surface, where there is warmth and light from the sun, has most life.

Predators and Prey

Many marine animals survive by eating other species. Some hunt large prey, while others scavenge remains and debris from the seabed. Ocean animals have developed ways to protect themselves from predators.

Many soft-bodied sea creatures are protected by a thick shell. The giant clam shuts its shell if it feels threatened.

GIANT OCEANIC MANTA RAY

MANTA BIROSTRIS
"TWO-NOSED BLANKET"

Habitat: Warm oceans; near the equator
Length: Male 4.5 m (14.8 ft); female 5.5 m (18 ft)
Weight: Male 1,300 kg (2,866 lb); female 1,600 kg (3,527 lb)
Diet: Shrimp, krill
Lifespan: Up to 80 years
Wild population: Unknown; Vulnerable

DID YOU KNOW? Sperm whales are the world's biggest predators at up to 20 m (60 ft) long. One sperm whale tooth can weigh 1 kg (2.2 lb).

The body can be up to 7 m (23 ft) wide.

Although they look like underwater birds, manta rays are fish. They feed on some of the smallest life in the sea—tiny invertebrates called plankton.

Microscopic Life

Plankton is a floating soup of tiny plants and animals. Some of the animals are the larvae (young) of jellyfish, crabs, and other invertebrates. Plankton is an important food for many sea creatures, from simple sea sponges to enormous whale sharks and blue whales.

Plankton includes tiny crustaceans called copepods. These two are clearly females because they are carrying sacs of eggs.

Fish

More than half of vertebrates are fish. These cold-blooded animals live in salt or fresh water, have tails and body fins, breathe through gills, and usually have scales. There are around 28,000 species, from the 12.65-m (41.5-ft) whale shark to a tiny swamp carp that measures just 8 mm (0.3 in).

Staying Safe

Many species limit the risk of being eaten by larger fish by sticking together in schools for safety. Other fish have amazing camouflage to avoid being seen. Speed and swimming prowess save the lives of some fish. Others have defensive spines, scales, or toxins.

Extraordinary Eels

Eels look more like snakes than fish. Long and thin, they move by wriggling. Eels are found in the sea and fresh water and most don't have scales. Some species can even move on land. Eels usually spend the day hiding in rocky crevices and come out at night to hunt.

The parrotfish is named for its beak-like mouth, designed for biting chunks of coral off the reef.

The puffer fish transforms itself if an enemy appears. It takes in enough water to double in size. The fish is suddenly ball-shaped, and covered with poison-tipped spines.

The giant moray eel is a predator that lives on coral reefs. It can grow as long as 3 m (9.8 ft).

At night, the parrotfish covers its body with slimy mucus. This hides its scent from nocturnal hunters.

The fish's gills are behind the cheek flap. They take oxygen from the water and produce waste carbon dioxide.

Moving the tail fin from side to side generates thrust. It propels the fish forward in the water.

STOPLIGHT PARROTFISH

SPARISOMA VIRIDE
"GOLDEN-HEADED GREEN FISH"

Habitat: Coral reefs; W Atlantic
Length: Male 50 cm (1.6 ft); female 30 cm (1 ft)
Weight: Male 1.6 kg (3.5 lb); female 1.4 kg (3.1 lb)
Diet: Coral polyps, algae
Lifespan: Up to 30 years
Wild population: Unknown; Least Concern

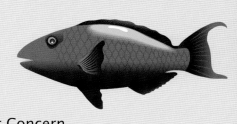

DID YOU KNOW? The ocean sunfish is the world's heaviest fish. Adults can weigh up to 1,000 kg (2,205 lb).

Sharks

Sharks are fish with skeletons made of tough, flexible cartilage instead of bone. They first appeared 220 million years before the dinosaurs. Today there are more than 500 species. Sharks have a reputation as fierce predators, but most species are harmless and shark attacks are rare.

All Shapes and Sizes

Most sharks— including the great white, tiger, blue, bull, mako, and reef sharks —have a sleek, streamlined body. Others are very different shapes. In deep waters, the frilled shark is long and eel-like, while the goblin shark is named for its unusual nose. The flattened bodies of angel sharks and wobbegongs suit life on the seabed.

The skin is as rough as sandpaper. It is covered with grooved, tooth-shaped scales that direct the flow of water over the shark's body and reduce drag.

The great white has an excellent sense of taste. It can detect a few drops of blood in the water from 5 km (3 miles) away.

There are ten species of hammerhead. These sharks have a T-shaped head with eyes far apart, which gives them a wide field of vision.

The shark has rows of sharp, triangular teeth up to 7.5 cm (3 in) long. As old ones are lost, new teeth move forward to take their place.

A torpedo-shaped body, pointed at each end, cuts down water resistance. The shark swims at 40 km/h (25 mph).

DID YOU KNOW? The Greenland shark is the world's longest-living vertebrate. It can reach nearly 400 years old.

Filter-Feeders

The three largest shark species— the whale shark, basking shark, and megamouth—do not hunt large prey. They take in water through their enormous, gaping mouth, and then force it out again through their gills. Their filter pads capture microscopic plants and animals from the water.

A whale shark's mouth is 1.5 m (4.9 ft) wide. It contains more than 300 rows of tiny teeth and ten filter pads for sieving plankton from seawater.

GREAT WHITE SHARK

CARCHARODON CARCHARIAS
"POINTED TOOTH"

Habitat: Oceans worldwide except the poles
Length: Male 4 m (13.1 ft);
  female 4.5m (14.8 ft)
Weight: Male 800 kg (1,764 lb);
  female 1,000 kg (2,205 lb)
Diet: Fish incl. sharks, turtles, marine mammals
Lifespan: Up to 70 years
Wild population: Unknown; Vulnerable

Cephalopods

Octopuses, squid, cuttlefish, and nautiluses belong to a group of animals called cephalopods ("head-foots"). Cephalopods have a large head, big brain, and a set of arms for gathering food. There are around 800 species. The nautilus is the only living cephalopod with a shell.

The octopus's head lies between the arms and body. It has well-developed eyes, a large brain, and a beak-like mouth. The octopus's poisonous saliva paralyzes prey.

Close Cousins

Octopuses and squid both have eight arms, but the squid also has a pair of tentacles that it uses to grab prey. Many octopuses spend their time on the seabed, where they eat crabs, clams, limpets, and scallops. Squid live in the open ocean and hunt fish, crustaceans, and other squid.

The giant Pacific octopus can change its reddish-brown skin to blend in with its surroundings.

OCTOPUS

OCTOPUS VULGARIS
"COMMON EIGHT FOOT"

Habitat: Warm oceans worldwide
Length: 60 cm (2 ft)
Weight: 5.5 kg (12.1 lb)
Diet: Fish, mollusks, crabs, other marine invertebrates
Lifespan: Up to 18 months
Wild population: Unknown; Least Concern

The body looks like a saggy bag. It contains the digestive system and three hearts. The octopus's blood is blue.

Facing Danger

Cephalopods camouflage themselves by changing the appearance of their skin. Many can also squirt a cloud of dark ink to confuse a predator while they make a getaway. Others protect themselves with venom. The tiny blue-ringed octopus contains enough to kill 26 humans in minutes.

Two rows of suckers on the arms help the octopus to hold, touch, and even taste. Each sucker has up to 10,000 nerve cells.

SWIMMING FIN

MANTLE

Water squirts from this funnel when the octopus is jetting through the water. The funnel also helps it to control direction.

Like octopuses, squid are jet-propelled— quickly pushing water from their mantle propels them forward. They also have a pair of swimming fins.

DID YOU KNOW? The colossal squid is the world's biggest cephalopod and the largest invertebrate. It is 14 m (46 ft) long and weighs up to 750 kg (1,650 lb).

Seahorses

A male leafy seadragon turns yellow to show it is ready to mate. It also changes for camouflage.

A horse-like head and snake-like tail make seahorses distinctive fish. Together with their close relatives, pipefish and seadragons, they form a family that contains around 230 species—of which 120 are found in warm, shallow waters off the coast of Australia. They eat tiny crustaceans and are well-camouflaged among plants.

Prehensile Tail

Seahorses are weak swimmers because they don't have the usual tail fin that pushes fish through water. They move by fluttering the small dorsal fin low down on their back. Easily swept away by strong currents, seahorses anchor themselves by wrapping their tail around a plant stem.

With its tail curled around a plant, this slender seahorse can take a break from swimming and rest.

When seahorse babies swim out of their father's pouch they are tiny, but fully formed.

Having Babies

Seahorse fathers give birth! The female lays as many as 2,000 eggs in a pouch on the male's belly. He provides oxygen and nourishment and, after about a month, the eggs hatch. Clouds of miniature seahorses swim off into the ocean. Only about one in 20 of these tiny fry will survive to adulthood.

Seadragons and pipefish swim horizontally through the water. Seahorses swim upright.

The seadragon's long, thin snout can suck up thousands of sea lice or other small crustaceans in a single day.

Leafy lobes disguise the seadragon so it looks like floating seaweed. They don't help it to swim.

LEAFY SEADRAGON

PHYCODURUS EQUES
"HORSE WITH SEAWEED SKIN"

Habitat: Ocean; S & E Australlia
Length: Male 25 cm (9.8 in);
  female 20 cm (7.9 in)
Weight: Male 114 g (4 oz);
  female 90 g (3.2 oz)
Diet: Plankton, small crustaceans
Lifespan: Up to 10 years
Wild population: Unknown; Least Concern

DID YOU KNOW? The dwarf seahorse is the world's slowest fish. Even at its top speed it travels only 1.5 m (5 ft) in an hour.

Crabs and Lobsters

There are more than 60,000 crustaceans, of which over 6,750 are crabs and 75 are lobsters. Prawns, barnacles, and woodlice are also crustaceans. Crabs and lobsters have ten legs and a tough exoskeleton—their shell—that protects their soft body. Each time they outgrow the shell, they shed it. There is a new, bigger one underneath.

The lobster has two compound eyes (eyes with many lenses) that sense changes in the light. Sight is not as important to a lobster as touch and smell.

The Y-shaped pair of smaller antennae can detect smells.

The long antennae help the lobster to feel its way and sense prey.

The lobster's larger claw is used for crushing prey and battling with other lobsters.

Land and Sea

Crabs can live in the sea, in fresh water, or on land. Land crabs have to return to the water to spawn (release their eggs). Lobsters are found only in the sea. Both crabs and lobsters are omnivores, feeding on a mix of plant and animal matter.

The blue land crab lives in an underground burrow. It eats leaves, fruits, grasses, and animal foods, including insects and carrion.

A hermit crab chooses its shell carefully so that it is a perfect fit. As it grows, it moves into bigger shells.

Moving House

Hermit crabs are unusual because they don't grow their own shells. They protect their soft body by moving into another creature's abandoned shell. Hermit crabs choose their shell carefully to be exactly the right fit. As they grow, they move into bigger shells.

AMERICAN LOBSTER

HOMARUS AMERICANUS

Habitat: Ocean beds; eastern North America
Length: 30 cm (12 in)
Weight: 500 g (1.1 lb)
Diet: Crabs, mussels, sea stars, other marine invertebrates
Lifespan: Up to 100 years
Wild population: Unknown; Least Concern

DID YOU KNOW? The Japanese spider crab is the world's largest crab. Its shell is 40 cm (16 in) wide and its legspan can be 3.6 m (12 ft) across.

Coral Reefs

Reefs are structures built up from the chalky casings of billions of tiny invertebrates called polyps. They are one of the world's richest habitats, home to about a quarter of all marine life. More than 1,800 species of fish inhabit the Great Barrier Reef.

Beneath this living colony of Acropora coral is stony rock. It formed from the old exoskeletons of dead Acropora polyps.

Hard and Soft

The polyps that build the reef are known as hard corals. When they die, they leave behind stony exoskeletons. New generations grow on top. There are also soft corals on the reef that can look more like plants. Both hard and soft corals form colonies in distinctive shapes. Hard corals have six waving tentacles to catch food; soft corals have eight.

Gorgonian, also known as the sea fan, is a colony of soft corals. Its flexible fan shape sways with the current. Gorgonian can be red, orange, yellow, pink, purple, or white.

CORAL SPECIES

HARD CORALS	SOFT CORALS
Blue coral	Dead man's fingers
Brain coral	Gorgonian
Bubble coral	Sea mat
Elkhorn coral	Sea pen
Great star coral	Star polyp
Pillar coral	Toadstool coral
Table coral	Tree coral

DID YOU KNOW? The Great Barrier Reef is more than 2,300 km (1,400 miles) long and can be seen from space. It is the biggest structure built by living creatures.

Smaller fish like these attract sharks and other predators to the reef.

Anemones are polyps attached to the reef. Their stinging tentacles catch and paralyze prey. Clownfish stay close to their host anemones.

Amazing Partnership

The reef is a dangerous place. The clownfish stays safe by living among the stinging tentacles of the sea anemone. Unlike most animals, the fish is immune to the anemone's toxins. In return, the clownfish cleans algae off the anemone, brings it food, and clears away any scraps.

The Deep

The deep ocean begins around 200 m (656 ft) below the surface and plunges to more than 10 km (6.2 miles). It is the largest but least explored habitat on earth. It is also dark and cold, and the water pressure is enough to crush an unprotected human. Animals that survive there are highly specialized.

Gulper eels are deep-sea fish with a huge gaping mouth. Their long, eel-like body stretches to accommodate any size of meal.

Deep-Sea Zones

The twilight zone reaches down to 1 km (0.6 miles). Many animals here have huge eyes to make the most of the light. Below this is the dark zone. Around 90 percent of the life here can produce its own light to find the way, communicate, or lure prey.

Birthplace of Life

The first single-celled life forms appeared around hydrothermal vents—holes on the seabed where heat and minerals bubble up from Earth's core. These bacteria survive without energy from sunlight. In turn, they support all sorts of life, including giant tubeworms, mussels, clams, shrimp, crabs, and fish.

The 2 m/7 ft-long tubeworms that live by deep-sea vents are simple creatures. They have no mouth, gut, or anus.

HUMPBACK ANGLERFISH

MELANOCETUS JOHNSONII

Habitat: Deep ocean; worldwide
Length: Male 3 cm (1.2 in); female 18 cm (7.1 in)
Weight: Male 50 g (1.8 oz); female 280 g (10 oz)
Diet: Fish, marine invertebrates
Lifespan: Estimated up to 3 years
Wild population: Unknown; Least Concern

DID YOU KNOW? The deepest part of the ocean, the Pacific's Mariana Trench, goes down 10,994 m (36,070 ft). It could swallow Mount Everest with 2.1 km (1.3 miles) to spare.

Only female anglerfish have a lure. Its glowing tip attracts prey or a mate.

Small fins cannot move the fish through the water at any speed. This ambush predator spends most of its time barely moving.

The humpback anglerfish eats crustaceans, snails, shrimp, and other fish. It can dislocate its jaws to fit in large prey.

Long, sharp, curved teeth can imprison prey unlucky enough to be caught.

Jellyfish

Jellyfish aren't fish—they are invertebrates from the same family as anemones and corals. They have been around for around 650 million years and live in every ocean. Instead of a brain, a jellyfish has a net of nerves that helps it detect changes in its surroundings and find prey.

Dangerous Jellies

Jellyfish are predators. They eat whatever they can fit into their mouth, including plankton, crustaceans, fish eggs, fish, and other jellyfish. They paralyze or kill their prey with venom produced by cells on their trailing tentacles. They also use their tentacles to push the food into their mouth.

Life of a Jellyfish

Jellyfish have complicated life cycles. Adults gather—sometimes in their millions—in breeding swarms called blooms. They release eggs and sperm into the water. The fertilized eggs must go through four different life stages before they become medusas (adults). Many are eaten and never reach adulthood.

The box jellyfish is the world's most poisonous animal. The stings of some species can kill a person in minutes.

In a bloom, sometimes the bigger jellyfish turn cannibal and eat the smaller ones.

Twenty-four long maroon tentacles trail behind the jellyfish. They have venomous stings.

Four frilly, creamy-white "arms" surround the sea nettle's mouth. Like the tentacles, they have stinging cells.

The main part of the jellyfish is called the bell. The mouth is hidden under the bell.

PACIFIC SEA NETTLE

CHRYSAORA FUSCESCENS

Habitat: Warm waters; E Pacific
Length of tentacles: 3 m (9.8 ft)
Width: 30 cm (1 ft)
Diet: Jellyfish, plankton, other marine invertebrates
Lifespan: Up to 6 months
Wild population: Unknown; Least Concern

DID YOU KNOW? Jellyfish bodies are 95 percent water. When jellyfish get stranded on a beach they quickly dry up and disappear!

Sea Stars

Sea stars first appeared in the oceans around 450 million years ago. Today there are around 2,000 species. Most sea stars have five arms, but the largest, the sunflower star, has up to 24. The sunflower star lives in the Pacific and weighs around 5 kg (11 lb).

Suckers!

The sea star's top surface has scaly skin covered with small spines. Its soft underside is hidden. The sea star clings to rocks or sand using the suction cups at the end of its feet. Even so, fish, crabs, sea turtles, and gulls all hunt sea stars.

On the underside of the sea star's body are hundreds of tiny tube feet. They are used for moving and catching food.

Most of a sea star's major organs are in its arms. It even breathes through its arms—the skin takes in oxygen from the water.

The purple sunstar's skin has protective, scratchy spines. This sea star hunts sea cucumbers, mollusks, and other sea stars.

ELEGANT SEA STAR

FROMIA NODOSA

Habitat: Indian Ocean
Width: 10 cm (3.9 in)
Weight: 35 g (1.2 oz)
Diet: Small marine invertebrates
Lifespan: Up to 5 years
Wild population: Unknown; status unknown

At the end of each arm is a simple "eye"—a cell that can detect light and dark.

The sea star can shed an arm on purpose, to distract a predator. It will regrow.

Coral Killer

The crown-of-thorns starfish is named for the long, thorn-like spines that protect the top of its body. It inhabits coral reefs in the Indian and Pacific oceans and feeds on coral polyps. A single crown-of-thorns starfish can eat its way through 6 sq m (65 sq ft) of living coral reef in a year.

The crown-of-thorns starfish's thorny spines are tipped with venom.

DID YOU KNOW? Once a sea star has prized open a clam, it turns its own stomach inside out and pushes it inside the shell to digest the clam's soft body parts.

Chapter Six

Minibeasts

Minibeasts are small invertebrates. They include an estimated 30 million insect species, as well as arachnids, such as spiders and scorpions, millipedes and centipedes, and worms. Some mollusks and crustaceans also count as minibeasts.

The woodlouse belongs to the same family as crabs and lobsters. It is a crustacean.

Count the Legs!

The word "insect" means "cut into pieces," and an adult insect always has three parts to its body—head, thorax, and abdomen. It also always has six legs in its adult form. A creepy-crawly with more or less than six legs is not an insect. Insects often have wings, but not always.

PRAYING MANTIS

MANTIS RELIGIOSA

Habitat: Fields, woods, grasslands; S Asia, S Europe, N America, Australia
Length: Male 6 cm (2.4 in); female 7.5 cm (3 in)
Weight: Male 2.5 g (0.09 oz); female 3 g (0.11 oz)
Diet: Insects, mantids, other invertebrates
Lifespan: Up to 9 months
Wild population: Unknown; Least Concern

The praying mantis shoots out its front legs to grasp insect prey, such as grasshoppers and crickets.

Recycling Machines

Minibeasts that eat dead plants and animals are known as detritivores. Earthworms, millipedes, slugs, and woodlice are all detritivores. They do a useful job in the food chain because they reuse nutrients, so these do not go to waste.

The shocking pink dragon millipede eats rotting leaves. It protects itself from predators by producing cyanide, a deadly poison.

The long body can be green, yellow, brown, or even black. It has two pairs of wings. Females cannot fly with their wings, but males can.

DID YOU KNOW? The smallest insect, a fairyfly, is smaller than a comma. It is a kind of parasitic wasp, and the female lays her tiny eggs inside other insects' eggs.

Spiders and Scorpions

Along with mites and ticks, scorpions and spiders are arachnids. There are at least 45,700 species of spider and 1,750 scorpions. They are eight-legged predators with no antennae or wings. All scorpions and most spiders have venom, but few are fatal to humans.

Super Spiders

All spiders spin silk, but not all build webs. From spiral orbs to tubes and funnels, spider webs are used to trap prey. Other spiders have different hunting methods. The trapdoor spider ambushes prey from a hidden lair, while the huntsman gives chase. Spiders range in size from a pinhead-sized orbweb to the massive goliath tarantula.

A crab spider has eight eyes to see in all directions. It lies in wait, perfectly disguised, ready to ambush insect visitors to the flower.

The leg–like pedipalps on either side of the jaws crush and tear up food.

The two front walking legs are also used to grasp bees, flies, and other prey.

The world's biggest spider, the goliath tarantula, can weigh 175 g (6.2 oz). It hunts mice, lizards, and small birds.

There are more than 2,000 species of crab spider. Many match the flowers where they hunt for insect prey each day.

Sting in the Tail

While spiders inject venom with their fangs, the scorpion produces venom from a stinger at the end of its curving tail. It stings to protect itself from predators. It can also stun struggling prey, but usually it saves its venom and kills prey with its powerful pincers.

Scorpions are tough survivors, found in many harsh habitats. This yellow fattail scorpion lives in deserts in North Africa and the Middle East.

CRAB SPIDER

THOMISUS ONUSTUS

Habitat: Moors, deserts, grasslands; Europe, Asia, Africa
Length: Male 4 mm (0.16 in); female 7 mm (0.28 in)
Weight: Male 2.5 g (0.09 oz); female 3 g (0.11 oz)
Diet: Small invertebrates
Lifespan: Up to 4 months
Wild population: Unknown

DID YOU KNOW? The giant huntsman has the largest legspan of any spider. At 30 cm (1 ft) across, it is larger than most dinner plates.

Beetles

A stag beetle lives just a few months as an adult. It spends up to six years as a larva, eating rotting wood.

A quarter of all the animals on Earth are beetles—there are about 400,000 species. These insects have two pairs of wings, but only the back pair is used for flight. The hard front pair acts as a protective shell. Beetles have four stages in their life cycle: egg, larva (grub), pupa, and adult.

Beetle Diets

Most beetles are plant eaters, but some are hunters. Fast-moving tiger beetles chase their prey. Most ladybirds consume aphids or scale insects. Ground beetles feed on maggots, worms, grubs, snails, and slugs. Dung beetles specialize in animal dung.

Leaf beetles eat plants. There are around 50,000 species, and many have striking metallic wing cases in blues, greens, reds, or yellows.

Strange Snouts

Weevils are the largest beetle family, with more than 60,000 species. They are plant eaters and have an especially long snout. Most weevils specialize in eating a particular kind of leaf, flower, fruit, seed, grain, or nut.

The giraffe weevil, named for its long neck, lives in Madagascar. It feeds on the leaves of a tree known as the giraffe beetle tree.

STAG BEETLE

LUCANUS CERVUS

Habitat: Hills, mountains; Europe, Asia, Africa
Length: Male 7 cm (2.8 in); female 4 cm (1.6 in)
Weight: Male 2.5 g (0.09 oz); female 4 g (0.14 oz)
Diet: Larvae: rotting wood; adults: nectar, tree sap
Lifespan: Up to 6 years
Wild population: Unknown; Near Threatened

Male stag beetles wrestle each other with "antlers" (modified jaws). The winner will mate with the female.

Sensitive antennae pick up vibrations, smells, and tastes. The beetle cleans its antennae regularly with its front legs.

Each of the stag beetle's six legs ends in a claw used for climbing and gripping.

The beetle's wing case is called an elytra. It forms a tough shell that protects against predators.

DID YOU KNOW? The world's smallest beetle is called *Scydosella*. It feeds on fungus and is no bigger than a grain of salt.

Slugs and Snails

Slugs and snails are gastropods, a kind of mollusk. There are around 75,000 species, and a third of these live on land. The others live in the oceans and in fresh water. Slugs and snails are found worldwide except in places of extreme cold. They have soft, slimy bodies and they move along slowly on a single, broad foot.

The spiral shell, made mostly of chalk, protects the snail from birds and other predators.

Almost the Same

Snails have a protective shell, but slugs do not. Slugs squeeze under logs or stones to stay safe and moist. Apart from that, slugs and snails are very similar. They feed mostly on plants and move slowly along a slime trail. They are also both hermaphrodite (part-male and part-female), so when they mate, each partner lays eggs.

The leopard slug eats dead plants and fungi, but also hunts other slugs.

COMMON GARDEN SNAIL

CORNU ASPERSUM "SPECKLED HORN"

Habitat: Gardens, farmland, meadows, forests; Europe, Asia, North Africa
Shell width: 3.5 cm (1.4 in)
Weight: 30 g (1 oz)
Diet: Plants
Lifespan: Up to 2 years
Wild population: Unknown; Least Concern

The radula (mouth) looks like a rough tongue. It is covered with tiny teeth for grating plant matter.

The snail has two pairs of tentacles. The longer two each have a simple eye at the end.

Sea Slugs

Nudibranches are marine snails but they are known as sea slugs because they shed their shell after their larva life stage. Many of the 2,300 nudibranch species are brightly patterned. Some just pretend to be poisonous and some really are—they may create their own toxins or take them in by eating other animals, such as sponges.

The variable neon slug is a nudibranch that lives in tropical waters. It grows to around 12 cm (4.7 in) long.

DID YOU KNOW? The African giant snail is the largest land–living gastropod. It is usually 18 cm (7 in) long and 9 cm (3.5 in) wide but can grow much bigger.

113

Butterflies

Millions of monarch butterflies spend winter in Mexico. They roost in fir trees.

Butterflies and moths are insects that feed on sweet, sugary nectar or fruit juice. There are about 180,000 species. Most moths are active at night and their wings are duller. Butterflies fly by day. Their antennae (feelers) are thin with a rounded end, while moths' antennae are feathery along their whole length.

Wonderful Wings

The wings of butterflies and moths are made of a hardened protein called chitin. They are covered with thousands of overlapping, powdery scales, so small they can only be seen under a microscope. The scales can be bright reds, oranges, yellows, or blues—all hues that help them to attract a mate or warn off predators. Others create mottled patterns that help the butterfly or moth to blend in with the background.

Swallowtails are named for their forked back wings. There are more than 550 species. This common yellowtail swallowtail is found across the northern hemisphere.

Monarch butterflies fly up to 4,750 km (3,000 miles) a year, migrating to and from their winter roost sites.

Adult butterflies sip nectar through tube-like mouthparts called a proboscis. When not in use, the proboscis coils under the head.

Adult monarchs are orange and black. They contain toxins from the milkweed plants they ate as caterpillars. Monarch caterpillars are yellow, black, and white.

Complete Metamorphosis

The eggs of butterflies and moths hatch into worm-like eating machines called caterpillars. A growing caterpillar splits its skin several times—each stage is called an instar. At full size, the caterpillar's body hardens into a shell-like pupa. Inside this shell, it breaks down and rebuilds itself. Then the pupa splits and the winged adult emerges.

The different stages in a Kentish glory moth's life

First instar

Second instar

Third instar

Eggs

Adult female

Pupa

Adult male

Like all insects, a butterfly does not have lungs. It takes in oxygen through "spiracles"—little holes on its thorax and abdomen.

MONARCH BUTTERFLY

DANAUS PLEXIPPUS

Habitat: Woods, gardens; N & C America, Australia, SE Asia
Wingspan: 10 cm (3.9 in)
Weight: 0.5 g (0.02 oz)
Diet: Larvae: milkweed; adults: nectar
Lifespan: Up to 8 weeks (6–9 months for ones that migrate)
Wild population: More than 100 million; Secure

DID YOU KNOW? Queen Alexandra's birdwing is the world's largest butterfly. Females have a 25-cm (9.8-in) wingspan. They live only in the forests of Papua New Guinea.

Bees

Worldwide, excluding Antarctica, there are about 20,000 bee species. Most live alone, but honeybees and bumblebees form large colonies, made up of a queen bee, hundreds of drones, and thousands of workers. The drones mate with the queen. The workers guard the nest, collect pollen and nectar, and care for young.

Breaking Away

When a bee colony becomes too large, the queen bee lays eggs that will develop into queens instead of worker bees. She leaves the nest with a large group of workers. The swarm flies to a suitable site to start a new colony. When they get there, the queen starts laying eggs already fertilized by the drones.

A swarm can contain hundreds or even thousands of honeybees.

Each leg is split into segments, so it is very flexible.

The bee has a pair of jointed antennae. They can touch, smell, taste, and pick up vibrations.

The bumblebee has two pairs of wings. They beat up and down so quickly that they make a buzzing noise.

GARDEN BUMBLEBEE

BOMBUS HORTORUM
"PLANT BUZZER"

Habitat: Grasslands, farmland; Europe, Asia, New Zealand
Length: 1.5 cm (0.6 in); queen 2 cm (0.8 in)
Weight: 2.5 g (0.09 oz); queen 4 g (0.14 oz)
Diet: Nectar, pollen
Lifespan: Up to 2 weeks; queen up to 1 year
Wild population: Unknown; Least Concern

Many plants need bees to pollinate them so that they can produce fruit.

Female bumblebees can sting. Their sting is not barbed like a honeybee's, so it can be reused many times.

Finding Food

Honeybees carry nectar and pollen back to the hive. They mix nectar with saliva to make honey to feed the young. When bees find a good source of nectar, they tell the other workers where it is with an elaborate, waggling dance.

The hairy body picks up grains of pollen, which rub off on the next flower the bee visits. This is called pollination.

Bees store honey in hexagonal cells, which they build from beeswax. The cells also house eggs and larvae.

DID YOU KNOW? A healthy queen bee can lay as many as 2,000 eggs a day.

The Grasshopper Family

Grasshoppers, locusts, and crickets belong to a group of insects called orthopterans ("straight wings"). There are at least 20,000 species, and more than half are grasshoppers. Orthopterans produce sounds by rubbing together their wings or legs. They have powerful back legs for jumping.

Searching for Food

Grasshoppers are active during the day and eat plants, while crickets come out at night and are omnivores. Grasshoppers are usually solitary but sometimes they band together in great swarms, usually when rains come and end a drought. Swarming grasshoppers turn from green to yellow and black. They are known as locusts.

When the cricket rubs together the upper and lower parts of its wings, they make a chirping noise.

There can be as many as 80 million locusts in an average swarm, and they eat their own weight in plants every day.

With its long back legs, this cricket is able to jump a distance of about 91 cm (3 ft).

Weird Wetas

Wetas are close relatives of crickets and are found only in New Zealand. There are more than 100 species, including tree wetas, giant wetas, ground wetas, tusked wetas, and cave wetas. Many do not have wings and none of them can fly. They hide during the day and feed at night.

The cricket's antennae are much longer compared to its body length than a grasshopper's.

The Mount Arthur giant weta is heavier than a mouse. There are ten other giant weta species across New Zealand.

The cricket's palps taste food and pass it back into the mouth.

The cricket's ear, or tympanum, is on its front leg. (In grasshoppers, the tympanum is on the abdomen near the back legs.)

SHORT-WINGED CONEHEAD

CONOCEPHALUS DORSALIS

Habitat: Saltmarshes, swamps, riverbanks, grasslands, farmland; Europe
Length: 15 mm (0.6 in)
Weight: Male 2.5 g (0.09 oz); female 4 g (0.14 oz)
Diet: Grass (seeds, buds, flowers)
Lifespan: Up to 1 year
Wild population: Unknown; Near Threatened

DID YOU KNOW? The biggest-ever swarm of locusts was in the American Midwest in 1875. It covered an area of 510,000 sq km (198,000 sq miles).

Worms and Leeches

Worms are invertebrates with long, thin bodies and no limbs. There are four families: ribbon worms, roundworms, flatworms, and segmented worms. There are more than 17,000 species of segmented worms, including all the ragworms, earthworms, and leeches.

Damp Environments

Worms and leeches need to stay moist so they do not dry out. Leeches live in lakes, rivers, and wetlands. Earthworms live in the soil. They keep soil in good condition and recycle leaves and other plants by eating them and producing rich droppings.

Freaky Flatworms

Tapeworms and other flatworms are the simplest worms. They do not have an anus so they use their mouth to get rid of waste as well as take in food. They move by gliding on small body hairs. Marine flatworms can also swim by rippling their body.

Each segment is covered with tiny bristles that help the worm to move and burrow.

Most leech species are predators that hunt other invertebrates. Some, such as this medicinal leech, feed on blood. They have a sucker at each end of their body.

The harmless purple flatworm (right) mimics a poisonous sea slug (left). It tricks predators into leaving it alone.

The tunnels that earthworms make let oxygen and rainwater into the soil.

The pale, lumpy section of the worm—the clitellum—contains its eggs.

The mouth sucks in soil and decomposing plants as the worm burrows.

The worm "breathes" by taking in oxygen through the slimy mucus on its skin. If its skin dries out, the worm dies.

EARTHWORM

EISENIA FETIDA
"SMELLY, DISCOVERED BY EISEN"

Habitat: Compost, leaf litter; worldwide except Antarctica
Length: 20 cm (7.9 in)
Weight: 8.5 g (0.3 oz)
Diet: Rotting plants
Lifespan: Up to 4 years
Wild population: Unknown; Least Concern

DID YOU KNOW? The bootlace worm is a very long ribbon worm in shallow seas. One that washed ashore in 1864 was a record–breaking 55 m (180 ft).

Ants

Ants are social insects that live in colonies. Each ant has its own job. The queen lays the eggs. Workers (smaller females) collect food and look after the nest. Some species have soldiers—larger workers that protect and expand the colony. The male ants' job is to mate with the queen. There are 22,000 ant species worldwide.

Weightlifters

Ants are omnivores. Workers find insects, seeds, nectar, and fruit to carry back to the colony. Army ants even transport much larger animals, such as lizards, scorpions, and small birds.

The antennae can pick up chemical messages called pheromones produced by other ants.

For their size, ants are the world's strongest animals. Wingless worker ants can carry more than 50 times their own bodyweight.

Two mandibles (jaws) at the front of the mouth can crush, slice, and bite. They move sideways, not up and down like human jaws.

Aphid Farms

Ants "farm" herds of aphids for their sugary honeydew. They stop the aphids escaping by biting off their wings or releasing chemicals that make aphids sleepy. The ants stroke the aphids' abdomens to make them ooze honeydew. The aphids also benefit because the ants fight off any predators.

This red ant is "milking" an aphid for its honeydew. Keeping aphid farms gives ants a ready supply of energy-rich food.

The ant can squirt acid from a gland at the end of the abdomen.

Ants do not have ears. A special organ near the knee makes sense of vibrations picked up from the ground by the feet.

Worker ants do not have wings. Only young queens and males have these so that they can fly away to mate.

BLACK GARDEN ANT

LASIUS NIGER
"HAIRY AND BLACK"

Habitat: Gardens, parks, cities; Europe, N America, Asia
Length: 4 mm (0.2 in); queen 9 mm (0.4 in)
Weight: 1 mg (0.00000004 oz);
   queen 12 mg (0.0000004 oz)
Diet: Nectar, small invertebrates,
   ripe fruit, human food
Lifespan: Up to 2 years; queen up to 20 years
Wild population: Unknown; Least Concern

DID YOU KNOW? Scientists believe that there are one million ants for every human. The world population of ants weighs more than the world population of humans.

Parasites

A parasite is any animal that lives on or inside another animal. Many parasites spend their entire life inside a host, while others feed off the hosts occasionally. Usually parasites do not kill their host, because then they would lose their source of food.

Outside In, or Inside Out

Many animals have parasitic worms. Tiny eggs laid in food or water enter the animal's body when it eats or drinks. The worms hatch in the intestines and live there. Parasitic wasps take no chances and lay their eggs inside a host. When the larvae hatch, they eat their host alive.

Many parasites are minibeasts, but not all. The sea lamprey is an eel-like fish that sucks the blood of other fish.

This host caterpillar is guarding fuzzy wasp pupae. The wasp larvae programmed it to do this by releasing special chemicals as they fed on its insides.

Hundreds of tiny teeth grip onto the host's flesh, while the tongue laps up blood.

Lamprey saliva contains a substance that stops blood clotting. This make its "meal" flow better.

Adaptable Fleas

Fleas are parasitic insects that use their amazing jumping power to move from one host to another. They feed on mammals' blood and their flat body is the perfect shape to move through hair or fur.

The cat flea is the most common of the 2,000 flea species. Despite its name it also sucks blood from dogs, foxes, raccoons, and skunks.

Sea lampreys are primitive fish. Like sharks, their bodies are supported by cartilage, not bone.

MALARIA MOSQUITO

ANOPHELES ALBIMANUS
"WHITE–HANDED AND USELESS"

Habitat: Close to water; C & S America
Length: 6 mm (0.2 in)
Weight: 12.5 mg (0.0000004 oz)
Diet: Larvae: water plants; adult males: nectar; adult females: blood
Lifespan: Male 2 weeks; female 4 weeks
Wild population: Unknown; Least Concern

DID YOU KNOW? The mosquito is the world's deadliest animal. Only females suck blood and pass on malaria, but they cause one million human deaths a year.

Glossary

AMBUSH PREDATOR
A hunting animal that waits in one place for prey to come close rather than hunting by speed or strength.

AMPHIBIAN
A cold-blooded vertebrate that lives in water as a larva and on land as an adult.

ANTENNA (pl: ANTENNAE)
One of a pair of sensory feelers on an invertebrate's head.

ARTHROPOD
An invertebrate with jointed legs, a segmented body, and an exoskeleton.

BACTERIUM (pl: BACTERIA)
A microscopic, single-celled organism, some of which cause disease.

BALEEN
A flexible keratin plate inside the mouth of some whale, which filters plankton from the water.

BLUBBER
A thick layer of insulating fat under the skin of some mammals that live in cold environments.

CARNIVORE
An animal that eats meat.

CARRION
A dead animal's decaying body.

CARTILAGE
A lightweight, flexible material that makes up the skeleton of some animals, such as sharks.

CEPHALOPOD
A marine mollusk with a large head and eyes and a ring of tentacles that have suckers.

CETACEAN
A marine or freshwater mammal with paddle-shaped forelimbs, no back limbs, and a flattened tail.

CHELONIAN
A reptile with a shell of bony plates and toothless jaws.

CLIMATE CHANGE
A long-term change in Earth's climate, especially a rise in average temperatures.

COMPOUND EYE
An eye that is made up of many small lenses, instead of just one.

CRUSTACEAN
An arthropod with two-part legs and a hard shell.

DETRITIVORE
An animal that eats decaying plants and animals.

DOMESTICATED
Tamed to live alongside humans.

ECHOLOCATION
A method of finding food or other objects by detecting reflected sounds.

EVOLVE
To change from one species to another over millions of years, by passing on particular characteristics from one generation to the next.

EXOSKELETON
A hard, outer skeleton.

EXTINCT
Describes an animal that has died out forever.

FERTILIZED
Describes a female cell that has combined with a male cell and can develop into a new living thing.

FILTER-FEEDER
An animal that eats small creatures by filtering them out of the water.

FOOD CHAIN
A series of animals, each of which depends on the next for food.

GILL
The organ that lets fish and some other underwater animals breathe by taking oxygen from the water.

GRAZER
An animal that eats grass.

HABITAT
An animal's natural environment.

HERBIVORE
An animal that eats plants.

HERMAPHRODITE
An animal that is both male and female.

HIBERNATE
To slow the body right down in winter in a kind of sleep.

HOST
An animal that provides the food for a parasite.

INCUBATE
To keep eggs at a steady temperature until they hatch.

INVERTEBRATE
An animal that has no backbone.

KRILL
A small, shrimp-like crustacean that is part of plankton.

LARVA (pl: LARVAE)
The young stage of an invertebrate that looks different to the adult.

LURE
Something that is used to tempt—for example, bring prey near.

MAMMAL
A warm-blooded vertebrate that has hair or fur and feeds its young on mother's milk.

MANDIBLE
The moving mouthparts of an invertebrate.

MARSUPIAL
A mammal that gives birth to underdeveloped young that carry on growing in a pouch on their mother's belly.

METAMORPHOSIS
The change from one form to another.

MIGRATION
A regular journey that an animal makes at the same time each year, for example to feed or breed.

MOLLUSK
An invertebrate with a soft, unsegmented body that lives in water or damp habitats. Many mollusks have an external shell.

MUSTELID
A mammal in the weasel family with a long body, short legs, and musky scent glands under the tail.

OMNIVORE
An animal that eats plants and meat.

OPPOSABLE THUMB
A thumb that can be placed opposite the fingers of the same hand to pick up or hold objects. All primates have this.

PARASITE
A living thing that does not produce or find its own food, but instead lives on a host that it relies on for food.

PHEROMONE
A chemical produced by an animal, which affects how other animals, often of its own species, behave.

PINCER
A claw that opens and closes.

PLANKTON
Microscopic plants, algae, and animals that float in the oceans.

POLLUTION
Damage to the environment from poisons and garbage produced by humans.

PREDATOR
An animal that hunts and eats other animals.

PREHENSILE
Able to hold and grasp.

PREY
An animal that is hunted and eaten by other animals for food.

PROBOSCIS
A sucking nose or mouthpart, often tube-like, that takes up food and water.

PUPA (pl: PUPAE)
An invertebrate in a hard casing that is changing from a larva to an adult. Pupae do not move.

RAIN FOREST
A thick, usually evergreen forest, often tropical, that receives more than 254 cm (100 in) of rain a year.

REPTILE
A cold-blooded vertebrate with dry, scaly skin that usually lays soft-shelled eggs on land.

SPECIES
One particular type of living thing. Members of the same species often look similar and produce fertile offspring together.

SPIRACLE
One of the tiny "breathing holes" on an invertebrate's body.

TEMPERATE
From the two regions on Earth between the hot tropics and cold polar regions.

TENTACLE
A slender, flexible organ used to sense, grab, or move around.

TERRITORY
The area that an animal defends against other animals, usually of the same species.

TUNDRA
Flat, treeless plains within the Arctic circle, where the ground is permanently frozen.

VENOM
A chemical that is injected into another animal to paralyze or kill.

VERTEBRATE
An animal that has a backbone.

WINGSPAN
The width of a flying animal's outstretched wings, from wing tip to wing tip.

Index

alligators 66, 84–85
ambush predators 70, 84, 101, 108, 126
amphibians 44, 66, 72–77, 126
anemones 99, 102
anglerfish 100–101
antennae (sing. antenna) 96, 111, 114, 116, 119, 122, 126
ants 122–123
apes 36–37, 38
arthropods 4, 106–111, 114–119, 122–123, 126
axolotls 77

bacteria (sing. bacterium) 100, 126
baleen 18, 126
bats 20–21
bears 12–13
bees 108, 116–117
beetles 4, 44, 75, 110–111
birds 4, 5, 9, 19, 20, 24, 25, 46–65, 80, 108, 112, 122
blubber 14, 17, 126
bowerbirds 55
butterflies 114–115

camels 34–35
camouflage 9, 15, 33, 83, 88, 93, 94
carnivores 6–25, 47, 126
carrion 7, 14, 50, 82, 97, 126
cartilage 78, 90, 125, 126
caterpillars 114, 115, 124
cats 8–9, 24
cephalopods 92–93, 126
cetaceans 18–19, 126
chameleons 80–81, 82
chelonians 78–79, 126
chimpanzees 36
clams 22, 86, 92, 100, 105
climate change 17, 126
compound eyes 96, 126
coral reefs 5, 88, 98–99, 105
crabs 4, 87, 92, 96, 97, 100, 104, 106
crickets 82, 107, 118–119
crocodiles 66, 84, 85
crustaceans 60, 87, 92, 94, 95, 96–97, 101, 102, 106, 126, 127

detritivores 107, 126
dolphins 18–19
domesticated animals 34, 35, 44, 126

eagles 24, 52–53
echolocation 19, 20, 21, 126
eggs 24, 43, 44, 46, 47, 49, 54, 61, 63, 65, 67, 74, 75, 85, 87, 94, 97, 102, 107, 110, 112, 115, 116, 117, 121, 122, 124, 126, 127
elephants 28–29, 30
evolution 4, 5, 20, 28, 46, 47, 57, 60, 126
exoskeletons 96, 98, 126
extinction 4, 10, 17, 38, 51, 64, 126

fertilization 75, 102, 116, 126
filter-feeders 18, 63, 91, 126

fish 86–91, 94–95, 98–99, 124–125
flamingos 62–63
fleas 125
flying foxes 20–21
food chains 107, 126
foxes 12–13, 53, 125
frogs 20, 66, 67, 72–75

gills 66, 77, 88, 89, 91, 126
giraffes 32–33
grasshoppers 107, 118, 119
grazers 26–27, 126
guanacos 35
gulper eels 100

habitats 5, 6, 10, 14, 15, 24, 33, 36, 42, 51, 52, 54, 57, 62, 77, 82, 84, 98, 100, 109, 126, 127
herbivores 26–37, 40–43, 126
hibernation 14, 78, 126
hoatzins 46–47
hornbills 4–5
hosts 99, 124, 125, 126, 127
hummingbirds 58–59
hyenas 6–7

iguanas 66–67, 71, 82–83
incubation 47, 65, 126
insects 4, 14, 20, 24, 25, 29, 36, 41, 48, 57, 59, 73, 76, 80, 82, 97, 106, 107, 108, 110–111, 114–119, 122–123, 125
invertebrates 4, 13, 18, 62, 82, 87, 92–93, 96–97, 98, 102–125, 126, 127

jellyfish 87, 102–103

kangaroos 40, 41, 84
koalas 40–41
krill 18, 60, 127

larvae (sing. larva) 66, 77, 87, 110, 113, 117, 124, 126, 127
leeches 120
lemurs 38
lions 8, 9
lizards 9, 20, 24, 66, 80–83, 108, 122
lobsters 96–97, 106
locusts 118, 119

mammals 5, 6–45, 48, 52, 82, 125, 126, 127
mandibles 122, 127
mandrills 38–39
manta rays 86–87
marsupials 40–41, 127
meerkats 24–25
metamorphosis 66, 75, 115, 127
migration 46, 58, 62, 79, 114, 115, 127
millipedes 106, 107
mollusks 92–93, 104, 106, 112–113, 126, 127
mongooses 24–25
monkeys 5, 38–39, 84
mosquitoes 20, 125
mustelids 22–23, 127

omnivores 14, 24, 26, 27, 39, 44, 97, 118, 122, 127
orangutans 36–37
ostriches 64–65
otters 22–23
owls 48–49

pandas 15
parasites 124–125, 126, 127
parrotfish 88–89
parrots 54, 56–57
peafowl 54–55
penguins 46, 60–61, 62
pheromones 122, 127
pigs 44–45, 82
pincers 109, 127
pinnipeds 16–17
plankton 18, 86, 87, 91, 102, 126, 127
polar bears 14–15
pollution 5, 17, 77, 127
praying mantises 106–107
predators 7, 10, 22, 24, 43, 57, 63, 65, 69, 70, 773, 6, 83, 84, 86, 88, 90, 93, 99, 101, 102, 105, 107, 108, 109, 112, 114, 120, 123, 126, 127
prey 6, 8, 9, 10, 13, 16, 18, 19, 22, 41, 48, 50, 60, 68, 69, 70, 71, 80, 84, 86, 91, 92, 96, 99, 100, 101, 102, 107, 108, 109, 110, 126, 127
primates 36–39, 127
pupae (sing. pupa) 110, 115, 124, 127
pythons 70–71

reptiles 20, 44, 66–71, 78–85, 126, 127
rhinos 30–31
rodents 42–43

salamanders 66, 76–77
scorpions 24, 25, 106, 108, 109, 122
sea lampreys 124–125
sea slugs 113, 120
sea stars 104–105
seahorses / seadragons 94–95
seals 16–17, 19
sharks 84, 87, 88, 90–91, 99, 125, 126
slugs 76, 107, 110, 112
snails 101, 110, 112–113
snakes 24, 66, 68–71, 84
spiders 4, 25, 76, 106, 108–109
spiracles 115, 127
sponges 4, 87, 113
squid 19, 60, 92, 93
squirrels 20, 42–43

Tasmanian devils 40, 41
tentacles 92, 98, 99, 102, 103, 113, 126, 127
territories 11, 23, 30, 54, 127
tigers 8–9
toads 66, 74–75
tools 22, 36, 56
toucans 54
tundra 42, 127
turtles 19, 66, 78–79, 84, 104

venom 24, 68, 69, 70, 71, 82, 93, 102, 105, 108, 109, 127
vertebrates 4, 6–85, 88–91, 94–95, 126, 127
vipers 68–69
vultures 50–51

wasps 107, 124
wetas 119
whales 18, 19, 86, 87, 126
wild boars 44–45
wildebeest 26–27
wolves 10–11
worms 27, 44, 66, 76, 106, 107, 110, 120–121

zebras 26–27